"Bonnie and Noel Drew's *Fast Cash for Kids* is an excellent how-to book for young people who want to start their own businesses but don't quite know how to begin. I have read the book several times now, and I can also say that it has given me a good many tips on how to sharpen my own teaching skills in the field of youth entrepreneurship. I highly recommend it."

Steve Mariotti, Founder and President
The National Foundation for Teaching
Entrepreneur ship, Inc.

"Kids are hungry for direction on how to take care of themselves economically. I think this book is what they are hungry for !!"

Joline Godfrey, Founder
An Income of Her Own

"Bonnie and Noel Drew's *Fast Cash for Kids* is a fantastic resource for young people and educators. It does more than just talk about making and managing money—it inspires young people to take action and learn through hands-on experience. We like it enough to offer it in the lobby of the world's only bank just for kids!"

Linda Sanders, President
Young Americans Bank and Education Foundation

"The next time your kids ask you what they can do to earn extra money, give them a copy of Bonnie and Noel Drew's *Fast Cash For Kids.* They'll get plenty of inspiration and ideas (handily arranged by job category), plus practical tips on how to write a business plan, get customers, and keep the books."

Janet Bodnar, Author
Kiplinger's Money-Smart Kids and Parents, Too!

"Junior Achievement is dedicated to helping young people learn the keys to success in America's free enterprise system. *Fast Cash for Kids* does just that. It offers students numerous ideas for businesses they themselves can manage, and easy-to-understand tips for making them successful."

Kathryn J. Whitmire, President and CEO
Junior Achievement, Inc.

"What a great book! It's a "must read" for every entrepreneur who has a child."

Wilson Harrell, Author
For Entrepreneurs Only

"*Fast Cash for Kids* makes my job as an educator easier! Students will enjoy the book because it is full of stories of young entrepreneurs. Teachers will love it because it contains a complete outline for an introductory course on entrepreneurship."

William W. Sherrill, Director
Center for Entrepreneurship & Innovation,
University of Houston

To our sons Jon and Robby and all the inspiring young entrepreneurs who have shared their stories in the second edition of *Fast Cash for Kids*.

· SECOND EDITION ·

FAST CASH FOR KIDS

BY

BONNIE AND NOEL DREW

Career Press
3 Tice Road
P.O. Box 687
Franklin Lake, NJ 07417
1-800-Career-1
201-848-0310 (outside U.S.)
Fax: 201-848-1727

A note before we begin:

The purpose of this book is to inspire the vision of entrepreneurship, give ideas for part-time business enterprises, teach the basics of a business start-up, and motivate young people to top performance.

The authors do not attempt to advise anyone on legal matters and make no guarantees that all principles taught in this book will be successful in every situation. The degree of success on any money-making venture depends solely on each individual. Those who undertake any business activity should contact appropriate city, state, and federal authorities for information on regulations, taxes, permits, and licenses. A qualified accountant, CPA, or lawyer should be consulted about tax and legal matters.

It is also the responsibility of the individual to follow proper health and safety precautions when using ideas suggested in this book. Parents should be aware of what their young people are doing and advise them closely on safety issues.

Fast Cash For Kids, 2nd Edition
ISBN 1-56414-154-3, $13.99
Cover design by Dean Johnson, Inc.
Printed in the U.S.A. by Book-mart Press

To order this title by mail, please include price as noted above, $2.50 handling per order, and $1.00 for each book ordered. Send to: Career Press, Inc., 3 Tice Road, P.O. Box 687, Franklin Lake, NJ 07417

Or call toll-free 1-800-CAREER-1 (Canada: 201-427-0229) to order using VISA or MasterCard, or for further information on books from Career Press.

Library of Congress Cataloging-in-Publication Data
Drew, Bonnie.
 Fast cash for kids / by Bonnie and Noel Drew.—2nd ed.
  p. cm.
 Includes index.
 Summary: Explains a variety of projects for children interested in earning their own money and learning how to manage a business efficiently and profitably.
 ISBN 1-56414-154-3
 1. Money-making projects for children—Juvenile literature. 2. Entrepreneurship—Juvenile literature.
[1. Money-making projects. 2. Business projects.] I. Drew, Noel.   II. Title.
HF5392.D735   1995
658'.041--dc20
                                                                    95-5746
                                                                       CIP
                                                                        AC

· TABLE OF CONTENTS ·

· INTRODUCTION ·

MONEY!

Just mention the word, rattle some change, pull out your wallet, and let a dollar bill float to the ground. What happens? Heads turn. Eyes open wide. Ears prick up. Hands perspire. Shoulders lean forward. Everyone is interested in what happens to money.

Why is that? The answer is simple. Money is how we get almost everything we need or want. Money is what we exchange for goods and services that keep us warm, give us shelter, keep us from being hungry, clothe us, and pay for our education.

Every young person knows it takes money to buy a hamburger, get in the movies, go on a ski trip, or buy a new car. Are you interested in money? Of course you are. Money is important to you.

When you're little, you start out getting money from your parents in the form of allowances, birthday gifts, tooth fairy money, and school lunch money. Occasionally you might be lucky enough to find some extra money or even win some money. But none of these sources is entirely satisfactory. Someone else is always in control of how much money you get!

As you grow older, you need a better source of income. Having your own money gives you more control of your life, more freedom to make choices, and more independence.

Smart young people have already figured out that the way to be more in charge of your life is to earn you own money. The problem is how. If you're under 15, you're too young to get a job. When you turn 15, most employers don't want to hire you because you have no experience. If you do get a job, it's for a bare minimum wage, and you have to work all the worst hours.

The young people you'll read about in this book have solved these problems by creating their own jobs. They've simply started their own business enterprises and employed themselves. They determine their own working conditions, set their own wages, and arrange their own time schedules.

Do they earn any money? Yes, some of them earn quite a bit of money. Even better, some of them discovered talents and chosen careers. Some have become well-known for their accomplishments. All of them have made their share of mistakes, but none is a failure, because they love what they do, and they are acquiring valuable skills for the future.

If you want to be part of this exciting group of young entrepreneurs, reading this book is your first step. The second edition of *Fast Cast for Kids* is all about how to earn your own money by finding a need in your community and filling it.

While you're learning to be your own boss, you'll also be preparing yourself for the future. You'll gain valuable experience in making decisions, handling money, managing time, and being a leader. You'll learn to analyze a business opportunity for cash potential, how to keep customers coming back for more, and how to think like an entrepreneur.

You'll have the satisfaction of saying, I did it myself. I'm my own boss. I make a contribution to this community, and I get paid for it.

And you'll deserve all the recognition and rewards you receive. Starting you own business is like going on a safari in Africa. You never know what to expect, but it's a great adventure for those who are brave enough to take the trip.

Happy hunting!

·1·

ARE YOU OPEN FOR BUSINESS?

WHEN CATHRYN MURRAY WAS 12 YEARS OLD, SHE LIVED IN A CRIME-RIDDEN AREA of Pittsburgh where there were lots of kids, but no stores or vending machines where kids could buy a snack after school. Cathryn knew kids loved sweets, so she decided to try an experiment. She took her leftover Halloween candy and started selling it to her neighborhood friends. Word spread quickly, and her limited supply was immediately gone.

Cathryn knew she had discovered a gold mine of opportunity. If she could find a way to supply the local kids with candy at a reasonable price, she would have all the spending money a 12-year-old girl in a ghetto could want.

With a little research, Cathryn found a warehouse outlet in town where she could buy candy at a low price. Then Cathryn's mother agreed to drive her to the warehouse once a week for supplies.

In a short time, Cathryn was earning a profit of $20 a day selling candy, chips, beef jerky, and other popular snack foods to all the kids in the neighborhood. Each day when Cathryn left for school, she carried a large duffle bag full of candy and snacks. Kids told other kids, and soon Cathryn was saving money to buy things she had always wanted.

OPEN For Business

Her first big purchase was a daybed for her room. But more important than that, the business provided Cathryn a regular income for school supplies, lunch money, and clothes all the way from sixth grade to ninth grade, when Cathryn and her mom moved from the ghetto to California.

CAN OTHER KIDS DO THIS, TOO?

Cathryn believes that anyone can start a business, no matter where they live. What's her advice to other kids looking for ways to start a business? With a smile, she simply says, "Go find a need and fill it."

That's too easy, you say. Isn't there a lot more to it? Actually, Cathryn's "find a need and fill it" advice is the backbone of industry and business today. Big business or small business, it makes no difference. We earn money when we find a need and fill it. This book will tell you how.

ADAM'S STORY

Adam Fingersh, a 17-year-old from Denver, discovered he had a talent for business when he was only 11.

It all started when Adam wanted to do something nice for his mom. So he designed and decorated a special T-shirt and gave it to her. His mom liked the shirt so much that she wore it to work. Her co-workers loved it and immediately wanted to know where they could get one, too. Soon, Adam could hardly keep up with the demand for his one-of-a-kind T-shirts. A new business, Adam F. Designs, was born.

Did Adam know there was a need for his wearable art? No, Adam just liked to be creative. He was simply expressing his talent when the ladies at the office went crazy about his T-shirts and demanded to know where they could buy one. Adam accidentally created a need for his product.

GETTING PEOPLE TO BUY

Could Adam (or any other young person) study what makes people buy and purposely create a need for a product? Of course. Big business does it all the time. They put samples of perfume in your magazine. You smell it, like it, and buy some the next time you go to the mall. They put samples of cereal in your mailbox. You taste it, like it, and next week your mom's got that cereal in her cart at the grocery store.

Young people can use these ideas to make money, too. As you read further, you'll learn more about the twin principles of business, "Find a need and fill it" and "Create a need and fill it," and how they can be used to your advantage.

ADAM'S BUSINESS EXPANDS

When Adam started Adam F. Designs, his first customers were the ladies at the office. But Adam was soon thinking of ways to expand. He wanted to sell his T-shirts in bou- tiques and gift shops all over Denver. To do this, he needed money for supplies.

Although his parents were supportive, Adam wanted to do everything on his own. So Adam went to the Young Americans Bank, where he had a checking and savings account, and asked for a loan.

The first thing the bank asked for was a business plan. Adam spent days construct- ing a written plan that told all about his business and how he could make enough money to pay back the loan.

The next thing the bank wanted was something for collateral. That made Adam ner- vous. The only thing he had to offer was his Apple computer. If he didn't pay back the loan, he'd have to give the bank his computer.

Adam took the risk and signed the papers. As it turned out, there was really no need to worry. Adam soon had agreements with several small shops to carry his painted T-shirts, jean jackets, and sweatshirts. By selling the T-shirts at $12 to $20 and the sweatshirts at $25 to $40, Adam paid off the loan in 2 months.

Adam F. Designs is now in its sixth year, and Adam has received many awards for his business talents. He won the National Entrepreneur of the Year award in the youth division in 1991. He has also served as chairman of the Youth Advisory Board at Young Americans Bank.

Adam is frequently asked to speak to other youth on how to be an entrepreneur. What does Adam tell all the other kids who want to start a business? "If you've got an idea, just try it. All you have to lose is your time. Giving up a few hours a day is worth the possibility of a lifetime of success."

WHAT MAKES A BUSINESS?

Lots of kids like Cathryn and Adam sell candy, paint T-shirts, mow yards, wash cars, or babysit to earn money. When does what you do to earn money officially become a business?

There is quite a bit of confusion about this question. Below are some interesting answers I've received from both kids and adults. Check whether you agree or disagree with each answer.

A business is a business when . . .

		Agree	Disagree
a.	You put up a sign.	_____	_____
b.	You get your first customer.	_____	_____
c.	You work more than one day a week.	_____	_____
d.	You hire employees.	_____	_____
e.	You file an income tax report.	_____	_____
f.	You get a license.	_____	_____
g.	All of the above.	_____	_____
h.	None of the above.	_____	_____

Some of these statements give clues about how a business becomes a business, but none of the above is correct.

FOUR CRITERIA TO DEFINE BUSINESS

The dictionary says *business* is "the selling of a product or service for a profit as a means of providing livelihood."

Looking closely at the definition, there are four criteria (or standards) that define a business: (1) the selling, (2) of a product or service, (3) for a profit, (4) as a means of providing livelihood.

To find out if you're in business, ask yourself these four questions:

	Yes	No
1. Am I engaged in selling?	_____	_____
2. Do I have a product or service?	_____	_____
3. Do I plan to make a profit?	_____	_____
4. Is the money for my use?	_____	_____

If your answer is Yes to all four questions, you have met the criteria for being in business. All that you lack is the mindset that says: "I'm open for business. I'm going to run my business like a business, because I am in business."

ME? I'M TOO SMALL!

Why is it so hard to see yourself in business? Because we have the idea that business has to be big. We think business is downtown, or in a big office building, or in a factory. It takes a change of thinking to see a youth-owned, part-time, money-making enterprise as being a business.

If you look closely at history, business hasn't been "big" for very long. Just 150 years ago, most business was conducted from someone's kitchen, living room, barn, or front yard. There were very few formal business establishments. Almost everyone ran a small business from home. Some baked bread, some made horseshoes, some sold eggs, some tailored suits, and some raised pigs.

Big business and industry are relatively new in history. And now we read in the paper almost every day that big business is downsizing because it got too big to run efficiently. Small business has always been the backbone of our economy and still employs more workers than all the big business in America put together.

WELCOME TO THE SYSTEM OF FREE ENTERPRISE

Be proud of what you do. If you're selling T-shirts, mowing yards, or shoveling snow, you're part of the free-enterprise system of America. You're using your own creativity, energy, and talent to produce products and services that benefit others. You are in business. So take your place in the economy. Call your business a business, and operate it like the best business in the world.

NOTES

·2·

How to Think Like
an Entrepreneur

YOUNG PEOPLE LIKE YOU, CATHRYN, AND ADAM WHO CREATE THEIR OWN BUSINESS enterprises are called *young entrepreneurs.* This chapter will tell you what that means and why it is so exciting.

You may already know more about being an entrepreneur than you think. Choose the best definition of the word *entrepreneur* from the list below.

An entrepreneur is . . .

    a. A side dish at a French restaurant.

    b. A person who interprets a foreign language.

    c. The manager of a large corporation.

    d. Someone who invents a business.

If you picked (d), someone who invents a business, you are right on target. An entrepreneur is an innovator or creator of business.

The word *entrepreneur* comes from the French word *entreprende,* which means "to undertake." The dictionary says an entrepreneur (ahn' tra pra nur) is "a person who organizes and manages a business undertaking, assuming the risk for the sake of profit."

THE SIX STEPS OF ENTREPRENEURSHIP

If you study the definition of *entrepreneur,* you will see six steps an entrepreneur takes to start a business.

INTERVIEW A LOCAL ENTREPRENEUR

Some of the business owners you know may be pioneers in their field of business. Make appointments to interview five business owners in your community. Use the interview questions below to guide your conversation. Your goal is to discover the spirit of entrepreneurship.

1. Where did you get the idea for your business? _____
   _____

2. How did you get started? _____
   _____

3. What obstacles did you have to overcome? _____
   _____

4. Who was your first customer? _____
   _____

5. How long did it take to make a profit?_____
   _____

6. Were you ever afraid you would fail?_____
   _____

7. What do you like best about your business? _____
   _____
   _____

8. How many hours a week do you work?_____
   _____

9. What can you tell me about success in business?_____
   _____

10. What advice do you have for a young person starting a business today?
    _____
    _____

An entrepreneur . . .

1. Sees an opportunity.

2. Organizes a plan.

3. Assumes the risk.

4. Starts the business.

5. Oversees management.

6. Intends to make a profit.

Cathryn and Adam practiced all six of these steps to entrepreneurship. These are the same six steps you will take as you read this book and embark on your own business adventures.

ENTREPRENEURS ARE TODAY'S PIONEERS

In my experience, entrepreneurs are even more exciting people than described by the definitions in this chapter. My favorite word to describe an entrepreneur is *pioneer.*

If you want to hear some inspiring stories, ask business owners in your community how they got started. You'll discover that some of your neighbors are pioneers in business. Many have overcome great obstacles to see their dreams come true.

Make a list of the five businesses you most admire in your community. Then call the owners and tell them you need some advice about a career in business. They will be glad to answer your questions. If you're not sure what to ask, use the interview form provided on page 8.

If you're lucky, you'll uncover a story of heroism or of great adventure. I promise you won't be bored. And you'll definitely discover that the American spirit of pioneering is still alive today. In fact, the spirit of pioneering and entrepreneurship is so alive today that the 1990s has been declared "The Decade of the Entrepreneur." Anyone, young or old, can be part of the movement. There is no age limit on entrepreneurship.

COPY SUCCESS

Experts have made many attempts to study successful entrepreneurs and tell us what they think and do. The truth is, no one absolutely agrees on what you have to be like to be an entrepreneur. The secret of learning to think like the most successful entrepreneurs in the world is this: *Observe what successful entrepreneurs do and copy them.*

Where will you find these entrepreneurs? You can start by reviewing the stories of Cathryn and Adam in Chapter 1 of this book. Next, remember recent conversations you had with business owners in your community. Then think about famous entrepreneurs in the news, or borrow some biographies of famous entrepreneurs from your public library.

WHAT DO YOU ADMIRE ABOUT ENTREPRENEURS?

Ask yourself this question: Who do I know who is an entrepreneur, and what do I admire about them? Here are some answers you might give:

1. They are self-confident.
2. They are enthusiastic.
3. They are goal setters.
4. They are creative.
5. They are determined.
6. They are hard workers.
7. They are open to new ideas.
8. They are independent.

There are many other qualities you might add to this list. Remember that entrepreneurs are not magic people who are born with all these characteristics. Most of them have developed these successful traits through experience. You can develop these characteristics, too.

Use the form that follows to evaluate your qualities of entrepreneurship. The purpose of this quiz is not to predict your rate of success in business. It is simply a tool to help you develop the traits of an entrepreneur.

HOW AM I LIKE SUCCESSFUL ENTREPRENEURS?

The statements below describe characteristics of successful entrepreneurs. After each statement, circle the number that comes closest to describing how often the statement is true for you.

1 = never true   3 = usually true
2 = sometimes true   4 = always true

1. I like to try new ways to do things.   1 2 3 (4)

2. I make decisions that are usually right.   1 (2) 3 4

3. I like to take charge and get things done.   1 (2) 3 4

4. I don't mind working hard to get what I want.   1 2 (3) 4

5. I enjoy accomplishing my goals.   1 2 3 (4)

6. I get energy from doing things I like.   1 2 3 (4)

7. I don't worry much about what others think.   (1) 2 3 4

8. I like to prove I can beat a challenge.   1 2 3 (4)

9. I like to plan my work before I get started.   (1) 2 3 4

10. I get along with most people I meet.   1 2 (3) 4

11. I like to be on time wherever I go.   1 2 (3) 4

12. I ask for advice when I need it.   1 (2) 3 4

13. I feel responsible to do what I say.   1 (2) 3 4

14. I tell the truth when I make a mistake.   1 (2) 3 4

If most of your circles are 3's and 4's, you are ready to enjoy becoming a young entrepreneur. However, you should look closely at the statements where you circled 2's and 3's. Are there some ways you can improve? Write your ideas for improvement on a separate piece of paper.

BELIEVE YOU'LL SUCCEED

The most important quality you must have as a young entrepreneur is belief in yourself. If you believe in yourself, you can learn everything else you need to know to be a success in business.

Remember this: Winners believe in themselves and keep one thought foremost in their mind—what I must do to succeed. Losers fear failure and keep one thought in their mind—how I can keep from losing. Success comes to those who believe they will be a success and simply go out and prove it.

ENTREPRENEURSHIP STARTS EARLY

Young people naturally possess many of the qualities of entrepreneurship. In fact, being young is often an asset in becoming an entrepreneur.

If you read stories of well-known entrepreneurs, inventors, artists, musicians, and world leaders, you will discover that many of them exhibited entrepreneurial talents at a very early age. There are numerous examples.

> Oprah Winfrey gave her first speech in public at age 2½. She decided she was going to earn her living talking when she was paid $500 to speak at a church when she was 12.

> Bill Gates, founder of Microsoft software company, started his first business at age 15. He and his friend Paul Allen wrote a traffic program called Traf-O-Data and made $20,000 before they ever entered high school.

Dave Thomas, Wendy's restaurant founder, started his career in the food service industry at age 15. Today he has over 4,000 restaurants in over 29 countries of the world.

Fred DeLuca, founder of Subway Sandwiches & Salads, started his first sandwich shop at age 17 to earn money for college. The chain has now grown to over 2,200 stores, with new shops opening at the rate of 20 to 30 a week.

Tracy Austin, tennis champion, was competing regularly against college students and adults when she was in first grade. By age 18, she had won over $1 million in prize money.

Debbi Fields, founder of Mrs. Field's Cookies, based her successful cookie empire on a recipe for chocolate-chip cookies she developed at age 13. Because the family grocery budget was often limited, Debbi saved the money she earned as a foul-line girl for the Oakland A's so she could buy butter instead of margarine to make toll-house cookies.

Marcel Bich, creator of BIC pens, sold flashlights door-to-door at age 18 because he intended to have a career in business and wanted to learn to be a salesman. Today his company sells 1 million BIC ballpoint pens a day in the United States.

You're the perfect age

Every young person has a valuable contribution to make to the world. Don't let any-one convince you that you're too young to follow your dream. You are the perfect age to become an entrepreneur, an inventor, a sports star, a politician, or anything else you want to be.

Here's why I believe now is the perfect time for you to become an entrepreneur:

1. You're old enough. You've had practice at being responsible both at home and at school.

2. You're ready to handle money. You may already have a bank account, and you like to set financial goals.

3. You're mature enough to understand and follow accepted safety practices.

4. You have plenty of extra time to devote to your business ideas.

5. You aren't risking your livelihood. If your business plans don't succeed right away, your parents are still there to provide a roof over your head and food to eat.

6. You're enthusiastic. When you have a goal, you use your energy to overcome obstacles and solve problems.

7. You're creative. Your fresh thinking often creates new products, services, and ideas.

8. You're young enough that adults still like to help you. (Most adults enjoy helping a hard-working young person.)

HOW DO I GET STARTED?

In this chapter, you've learned a great deal about what it means to be an entrepreneur. The chapters to follow will guide you through the actual start-up of your own business enterprise.

As a young entrepreneur, you will:

1. See opportunity.

2. Organize a plan.

3. Assume the risk.

4. Start the business.

5. Oversee management.

6. Make a profit.

The first step is learning to see money-making opportunity everywhere you go. That process begins in Chapter 3.

·3·

How to Find a Money-Making Idea

EVERY BUSINESS ENTERPRISE, BIG OR SMALL, STARTS AS A SINGLE THOUGHT IN THE mind of the entrepreneur. Cathryn Murray had an idea that her neighborhood friends would buy leftover Halloween candy. Adam Fingersh had an idea for creating new T-shirt designs. Many well-known corporations and products we use daily were created by ordinary people who simply had an idea. Let's look at some examples.

FIRST COIN-OPERATED VIDEO GAME

Nolan Bushnell, today known as the founder of Atari and father of the entire video game industry, worked as manager of game concessions for an amusement park while he was in college. He loved games so much that he often played cards and pinball machines instead of studying.

When Nolan graduated from college in 1968, he had an idea for a way to apply computer technology to pinball machines. However, when Nolan proposed his first coin-operated computer video game in 1972, experts in the industry laughed at the idea. They didn't believe anyone would sit in front of a TV screen and play a game that involved only pushing buttons.

Nolan was sure his idea was a winner. He and his partner, Ted Dabney, each invested $250 and started manufacturing the first game (Pong) on their own. They had so little money that Nolan got a pinball machine route so they could buy parts. Four years later, in 1976, the Atari Company was so successful that Warner Communications bought them out for $28 million.

MIX-AND-MATCH SPORTSWEAR

Liz Claiborne started working in the New York fashion industry when she was 19. For 25 years she designed clothing for various companies and gradually developed a reputation as one of New York's top designers. In the early 1970s, she tried to convince the company she was working for that it should introduce a line of mix-and-match separates for the upscale business woman. No one would listen to her idea.

In 1976, Liz Claiborne formed her own company and produced her first line of mix-and-match sportswear coordinates. First year's sales totaled over $2.5 million. Since that time, Liz Claiborne fashions have completely revolutionized and dominated the entire women's wear industry. *Fortune Magazine* has declared that "Liz Claiborne is America's most successful female entrepreneur."

SMELLY CREAM BECOMES COSMETIC INDUSTRY

Mary Kay Ash was a single mother trying to support three children in the early 1950s by selling Stanley Home Products. One night at a Stanley party she met a group of women who had the most beautiful skin she had ever seen. Inquiring about their secret, she discovered that the women were using a special hide-tanning cream developed by the hostess's father, who was a leather tanner.

Years later, in 1963, Mary Kay was sitting at her kitchen table thinking about a book she wanted to write about, how the business world could be improved. Suddenly, she had an idea that she should forget about the book and start the "dream company" she had envisioned for so many years. That day was the birthday of Mary Kay Cosmetics.

Looking for a product to market, Mary Kay purchased the rights to the smelly hide-tanning cream she had discovered years before and turned it into a line of skin-care preparations. The fourth year she was in business, sales exceeded $1 million. Today Mary Kay Cosmetics is the largest direct-sales multilevel marketing cosmetics firm in the world, with over 250,000 sales consultants in 19 countries and sales of over $1 billion.

RESEARCH PAPER BECOMES FEDERAL EXPRESS

Fred Smith was a student at Yale University in the mid-1960s. While doing research for a course in economics, he formulated an idea for an overnight package delivery system that would service the entire United States. His professor said the proposal was very poorly thought out and was full of critical errors in planning. He received only a "C" on the paper, but graduated anyway.

Five years later, after serving as a fighter pilot in Vietnam, Fred Smith started the Federal Express company using the same ideas he had written about in college. The first years were difficult because big business did not immediately see the value of overnight delivery. But his plan eventually worked, and Fred Smith changed the package delivery business in the U.S. forever. Federal Express has since grown to employ over 50,000 people and deliver over 150 million packages overnight every year.

THE IMPORTANCE OF IDEAS

Ralph Waldo Emerson once said, "There is no prosperity...or great material wealth of any kind, but if you trace it home, you will find it rooted in a thought of some individual." You and I might rephrase Mr. Emerson's words this way: Nothing in business happens until someone has an idea. So where do entrepreneurs get their ideas? This chapter answers that question.

ENTREPRENEURS ARE "OPPORTUNITY SEEKERS"

Most entrepreneurs practice the habit of watching for money-making ideas everywhere they go. They are always on the lookout for opportunity.

The dictionary defines *opportunity* as a time or occasion that is right for doing something—a good chance. So young opportunity seekers are looking for times or occasions that are right for earning money.

SECOND-GRADER RECOGNIZES OPPORTUNITY

Claire Randall of Galveston, Texas, was in second grade when she saw her first money-making opportunity. That year, her parents had purchased a computer for the family. At first, Claire only used the computer to play games. But soon she felt more confident and started using the computer to make her own birthday party invitations and name tags for Christmas gifts.

One day at school, a girl showed Claire her dad's new business card. Thinking like an opportunity seeker, Claire said to herself, "That's easy. I can do that on my computer."

The next day Claire returned to school with a surprise. She had made business cards for her friend. Soon other kids wanted cards, too, and Claire was suddenly in business.

Every day at school, Claire took orders. In the evenings she designed the cards. Most of her classmates liked cards with their name only and a picture symbolizing their hobby or special interest. They were all quite willing to pay Claire's price of eight cards for $1.

WHEN OPPORTUNITY KNOCKS, MAKE A HABIT OF LISTENING

Lots of people have computers, and lots of people carry business cards. Why did Claire combine these two factors to invent a new business?

Claire was very observant. When her friend displayed her dad's business card, Claire saw more than a business card. She saw a second-grade girl who was impressed with her dad's business card. That was different. Claire's entrepreneurial mind flashed the idea: Business cards for kids. Do it! So she did, and it worked.

Kemmon Wilson, founder of Holiday Inn, had a favorite saying about looking for opportunity. He said, "Opportunity comes often. It knocks as often as you have an *ear* trained to hear it, an *eye* trained to see it, a *hand* trained to grasp it, and a *head* trained to use it."

Looking for opportunity is not something you do just once. You make it a habit. If you are willing to practice a little, you can become very skillful at recognizing opportunities other people don't see. After a while, you will begin to recognize opportunity everywhere you go.

SIGNS OF MONEY-MAKING OPPORTUNITY

What would you do if I told you there was a $20 bill laying in your front yard? (Choose an answer.)

a. Stay in the house and watch TV.

b. Argue with your sister about whose job it is to pick up money in the front yard.

c. Beat everyone out the front door so you can be first to find the $20.

Of course you would immediately rush out and find that $20. Why ask such a silly question? Because your neighborhood is full of $20 bills just waiting for you.

No, there probably aren't any $20 bills laying in front yards. You'll find the $20 bills I'm talking about in the form of money-making opportunities: yards to mow, cookies to bake, pools to clean, pets to groom, or children to help with math.

Watch for these five signs of money-making opportunity in your neighborhood:

1. *Look for things people are too busy to do.* We live in a busy world. People don't have time to iron shirts, polish furniture, paint fences, bake birthday cakes, or decorate for holidays. Look for services that will give your customers more time to enjoy life.

2. *Look for things people don't like to do.* Everyone has chores they hate: washing windows, pulling weeds, cleaning the oven, bathing the dog, or organizing the garage. Specialize in taking care of a job no one likes to do, and you will always have plenty of customers.

3. *Look for things that get dirty over and over.* Almost everything gets dirty: cars, boats, pools, parking lots, driveways, golf clubs, floors, bathrooms. Cleaning is a money-making opportunity that can never be used up.

4. *Look for things people throw away.* Outgrown clothes, toys, books, puzzles, games, household items, and recyclables are great for garage sales, toy sales, book sales, or recycling projects. These money-making enterprises are good for our environment and our community.

5. *Look for ways to use your special talent or experience.* Create your own business based on something you do well. You might build skate ramps, start a band, give dog obedience lessons, teach Spanish,

MASTER LIST OF MONEY-MAKING OPPORTUNITIES

Date	Location	Idea	Possible Earnings

Clues to watch for:

1. Things people are too busy to do
2. Things people don't like to do
3. Things that get dirty over and over
4. Things people throw away
5. Ways to use a special talent or experience

or specialize in helping the elderly. Getting paid to do something you enjoy is like getting paid to have fun.

HOW TO CAPTURE OPPORTUNITY

Nolan Bushnell, Liz Claiborne, Mary Kay Ash, and Fred Smith are all famous entrepreneurs today. But at one time they were young people sitting in a classroom wondering what they were going to do in the future. Their businesses all started the same way—as a single idea in the mind of the entrepreneur. They eventually earned millions with their ideas. But who's to say you won't have an idea that's just as big? I believe it's possible.

Capture Good Ideas!

As an enthusiastic young entrepreneur, you may have hundreds of ideas for starting a business. Unless you have a way to capture these ideas on paper, many of your opportunities may be lost or forgotten forever. It is very important that you develop the habit of keeping a master list of all your good ideas.

Use the form on page 20 to start your master list of money-making opportunities. Then go for a walk in your neighborhood and look for the five signs of money-making opportunity listed in this chapter. As you spot these opportunities, write them on your list.

IS IT POSSIBLE TO RUN OUT OF OPPORTUNITY?

Opportunity is constantly changing. Winter opportunities disappear as spring arrives. Summer opportunities are different from fall opportunities. Jobs that need to be done this week may not be available next week. But you will never run out of ideas to add to your opportunity list. There will always be *new* money-making opportunities to replace those that are used up.

USE THIS BOOK AS A CATALOG OF OPPORTUNITY

If you need help getting started on your list of money-making opportunities, take a few moments to browse through the rest of this book. You will find over 101 business ideas for young entrepreneurs. You can use the business ideas in *Fast Cash for Kids* three ways:

1. Create the business exactly as described.

2. Adjust details to customize the business for you.

3. Combine multiple ideas to make a bigger business.

Add the ideas you like best from this book to your master list of money-making opportunities. Most young entrepreneurs find they have so many good ideas they can't possibly take advantage of them all. Your next step will be to choose the right business opportunity for you.

· 4 ·

How to Choose the Right Business for You

SHANE WILSON, 14, FROM CYPRESS, TEXAS, LIKES GETTING PAID TO HAVE FUN. WHAT is his business? It's The Magic of Shane-O.

Three years ago, right at the end of sixth grade, Shane discovered that his mom had enrolled him in a summer magic class. At first Shane thought the class would be boring. But he was wrong. Learning to do magic tricks with balloons, cards, handkerchiefs, and other props was the most fun Shane ever had.

Shane loved performing magic so much that he practiced for hours. He learned to do balloon sculptures and was soon earning $40 for appearing at children's birthday parties. Kids at school constantly asked him to do card tricks. And relatives began recommending The Magic of Shane-O for company Christmas parties.

Today Shane finds every minute he can to practice new tricks, advance his skills, and improve his showmanship. No one makes him spend hours in front of a mirror. No one forces him to perform. He has discovered what I call the WOW Factor in entrepreneurship. He can work longer, harder, and with more enthusiasm than anyone else because he is totally in love with his work. He's getting paid to have fun.

FIND SOMETHING YOU LOVE

Harvey Mackay, one of America's most well-known entrepreneurs, said, "Find something you love to do and you'll never have to work a day in your life."

Successful entrepreneurs do not hate their work. They choose businesses that allow them to do work they love. You and I may think these people are working, but they aren't. They are having fun.

On pages 25 and 26 you will find a personal survey titled "What Kind of Business Would I Enjoy?" This survey will help you discover the kind of work you like best. Answer the questions as completely and honestly as you can. The more you know about yourself, the more accurate you will be at choosing money-making opportunities that are right for you.

After you have completed your personal survey, make some extra copies and ask several friends or relatives to answer the survey about you also. Their input may help you see potential interests and skills you've overlooked.

BE HAPPY WITH YOUR WORK

If you want to enjoy your work, choose opportunities that allow you to do what you love. You are only limited by your imagination. Here are some examples:

If you like children, you could put on puppet shows, be a birthday clown, or teach crafts.

If you like working outdoors, consider painting house numbers on curbs, cleaning pools, or landscaping.

If you prefer indoor jobs, start a baking service, teach music lessons, or specialize in cleaning closets.

If you love animals, try a pet photography business, raise tropical fish, or offer flea baths for dogs.

If you enjoy computers, you can offer word-processing services, print banners for garage sales, or publish a neighborhood newsletter.

PERSONAL SURVEY
WHAT KIND OF BUSINESS WOULD I ENJOY?

What I like:

(List hobbies, clubs, sports, special interests.)

1. _Gymnastics_
2. _Horses_
3. _Being silly_
4. _____
5. _____

What I do well:

(List skills such as art, cooking, computer, etc.)

1. _computer_
2. _Reading_
3. _Coloring_
4. _____
5. _____

Work experience:

(List jobs you have done before and liked.)

1. _AlPabetizing Files_
2. _____
3. _____
4. _____
5. _____

PERSONAL SURVEY

(Circle the appropriate answer.)

1. I like to sell things.   (yes)   no

2. I have a driver's license.   yes   (no)

3. I like to
   a. work with others.   (b.) work independently.

4. I like to
   a. work with people.   (b.) work with things.

5. I like to
   a. work indoors.   (b.) work outdoors.

6. I like
   a. lots of physical activity. (b.) being still.

7. I like
   (a.) a variety of tasks.   b. repeating tasks.

8. I don't mind getting dirty
   when I work.   (yes)   no

9. I like thinking up new ideas. (yes)   no

10. I like taking care of the details. (yes)   no

STEP 1: CREATE A LIST OF BEST IDEAS

How many of the ideas on your master list of money-making opportunities match your special talents and abilities?

Take a highlighter pen and review your master list of money-making ideas. Highlight only the ideas that match your answers on the personal survey. Then transfer the highlighted ideas to a new list titled "Best Ideas for Me."

If you have carefully considered your opportunities, you now hold a very exciting list in your hands—your personal Best Ideas list. These are the current business ideas that offer you the greatest potential for satisfaction and success as a young entrepreneur. These are opportunities you would enjoy exploring further. Perhaps one of them is a rare WOW Factor idea.

STEP 2: MEASURE THE POSSIBILITIES

Smart entrepreneurs base their choice of a money-making opportunity on many factors. The first question they ask is: Would I enjoy it? But equally important are questions about the possible success of the business idea. The entrepreneur studies the facts and asks, Will it work? Is it a *feasible* idea?

The dictionary defines *feasibility* as "capable of being carried out." Another word for *feasible* is *possible.* Before you make a final decision about a business opportunity, you need to ask: Is it possible?

Take time to study carefully the opportunities on your Best Ideas list. Use the feasibility checklist shown on page 28 to analyze each opportunity. Cross off the ideas that are least feasible—those that seem least likely to be a success.

STEP 3: CONSIDER THE PROFITS

When you get down to only two or three ideas on your Best Ideas list, the decisions get harder. All of the ideas may be full of possibility and sound like lots of fun. But since you need to decide on one idea for now, break the tie by considering the overall profitability. These are the questions to ask:

1. Which requires the least risk?
2. Which is the fastest to get started?
3. Which will bring the greatest income?

FEASIBILITY CHECKLIST

Before you choose a business, use the questions on this checklist to evaluate your money-making ideas. If any of your answers are No, use the blank space beneath that question to tell how you might overcome that obstacle.

1. Is it honest?   Yes____   No ____

2. Is it legal?   Yes____   No ____

3. Is it safe?   Yes____   No ____

4. Is there a demand for the product?   Yes____   No ____

5. Do I have a source of start-up money?   Yes____   No ____

6. Do I have access to equipment?   Yes____   No ____

7. Will I need permits or licenses   Yes____   No ____

8. Do I have adequate training?   Yes____   No ____

9. Do I have enough time?   Yes____   No ____

10. Will I need help doing the work?   Yes____   No ____

11. Will I need transportation?   Yes____   No ____

12. Can I make enough profit?   Yes____   No ____

If you don't know the answers to some of these questions, ask for help. Good sources of help are the Chamber of Commerce, your homeowner's association, parents, teachers, and other business owners in the community.

USE THIS SYSTEM AGAIN

If you have followed the step-by-step instructions in this chapter, you have now selected the one best money-making opportunity for you. And you can use this same system for choosing opportunity again and again as new opportunities arise throughout your career as an entrepreneur.

An easy way to summarize this system is to remember three questions: Will I enjoy it? Is it feasible? Is it profitable? Each time an idea pops into your head, quickly evaluate the opportunity by asking your three questions. You will become very accurate at discarding ideas that are a waste of time. And you will become very good at recognizing opportunities that are right for you.

FOLLOWING YOUR DREAM

Deciding on a business venture is an exciting moment in your life. It is a moment of commitment to a goal. It's a time when you can most clearly envision future success.

One way to capture your enthusiasm is to write your dreams and goals down in the form of a letter to yourself. Describe the business as if you were writing to your best friend. Tell why you believe it's going to be a success and what you're going to do to make it work. Get as much of your dream on paper as possible. Moments of inspiration are rare and should be regarded as highly significant.

DON'T STOP NOW

This chapter has been your guide to selecting the right money-making opportunity for you. But it takes work to turn good ideas into fast cash. You will not earn a penny if you stop here. Chapter 5 will tell you how to take the action steps necessary to make your business a success.

NOTES

·5·

HOW TO TURN YOUR IDEA INTO A BUSINESS

LIZA WANZEK, AGE 15, AND LARAE WANZEK, AGE 17, ARE COUSINS WHO LIVE IN A semirural area just outside Jamestown, North Dakota. Three years ago they signed up for a 10-week class called "Be Your Own Boss" taught by local 4-H leaders. At the end of the 10 weeks, Liza and LaRae had become business partners with a complete written plan of how they would organize and operate a business called Lunch Box on Wheels, a portable catering service.

With their business plan in hand, Liza and LaRae applied for and received two small grants for $150 and $300 and a loan for $200. They used the money to buy supplies and equipment, have flyers and business cards printed, and get their business started. Since neither of the girls were old enough to drive, their parents took turns providing transportation. But Liza and LaRae did all the menu planning, cooking, serving, and clean up.

Today their best customers are auctioneers, cattle buyers, and local ranchers who happily pay $2 a plate for barbecue sandwiches, chili dogs, or tacos while attending auctions, horse shows, or public events catered by Lunch Box on Wheels. They get most of their bookings through word-of-mouth advertising and flyers placed on local bulletin boards.

When Liza and LaRae have a large event to cater, they use their charge account at the county market or money from their joint savings account to buy supplies. They pay all bills within 30 days and operate a completely debt-free business.

HOW DID THEY DO THAT?

The business plan Liza and LaRae wrote 3 years ago is the foundation of their operation and success. It tells them exactly how much they have to charge for every candy bar or sandwich in order to make a profit. Liza and LaRae update their business plan constantly with records of every event they cater, new menus, recipes, price comparisons, profit-and-loss statements, and plans for future improvements.

WHY BOTHER PLANNING?

Young entrepreneurs are delightfully enthusiastic. When they think up an exciting new idea to earn money, they often go straight out the door and start getting customers. They usually enjoy taking risks and don't mind solving problems or making up answers as they go along. As a result, you often hear them say things like this:

> So what if I've never baked chocolate-chip cookies in my life! Anyone can follow the directions on the package, can't they?

> You mean I'm supposed to pay for the gas for the lawnmower? I thought you were going to do that!

> I can't believe the homeowner's association says we need a permit to sell lemonade in front of our house! It's our property, isn't it?

A BUSINESS PLAN PROVIDES STRUCTURE

It may sound like fun to be a free-wheeling entrepreneur with dollar bills stuffed in your pockets and customers on every street corner, but this haphazard way of doing business rarely succeeds for very long. Sooner or later, you start losing jobs because you can't remember who you promised what or when you're supposed to be where.

Do you remember playing with blocks when you were little? Each kid in the class always tried to build the highest tower of blocks. After a while, you learned that you could build a higher tower if you started with a broader base.

Building a business is a lot like building a tower of blocks. Each block represents a component of the business. The more time and blocks you spend laying the base, the higher you can go toward your goals.

Your business plan is the structure or base of the business. Some entrepreneurs think of the business plan as a road map that helps you arrive at a destination. However you like to think of it, the business plan is not just a document that you write. It is a plan that you follow.

These are the purposes of writing a business plan:

1. To get a clearer picture of your business
2. To see if your idea will really work
3. To plan details you might overlook
4. To provide structure for operations
5. To set goals
6. To explain your business to others
7. To apply for a loan (if you need one)

WHAT A BUSINESS PLAN INCLUDES

There are many textbooks and business manuals that tell how to write a business plan. Some go into great detail and require pages and pages of writing. Others are very simple. The truth is, there is no absolute set way a business plan must be written. There are, however, three basic topics every business plan should cover. These topics are: organization, marketing, and finance. In a way, the business plan is actually three plans in one:

1. The Organizational Plan
2. The Marketing Plan
3. The Financial Plan

These three "mini-plans" are combined to form a master document we call the *business plan*.

This chapter contains the guidelines for writing Part 1: The Organizational Plan. If you aren't sure what some of the terms mean, read further in the chapter. Each term will be explained.

GUIDELINES FOR WRITING THE BUSINESS PLAN
PART 1: THE ORGANIZATIONAL PLAN

Use this checklist as a guide for writing Part 1 of your business plan. A space has been provided for you to check off the questions as you complete the answers. All of the questions are explained in detail later in this chapter.

A. Define the business.

_____ 1. What is your business name?

_____ 2. Where is your business located?

_____ 3. What is the purpose of your business?

_____ 4. What are the legal requirements?

_____ 5. Who are the key people in your business?

_____ 6. How much time will you invest?

_____ 7. What are your goals for the future?

B. Describe the product.

_____ 8. What are your products or services?

_____ 9. What are the advantages of your product?

_____ 10. How do you produce what you sell?

C. List your resources.

_____ 11. How much cash are you investing?

_____ 12. What equipment will be used in the business?

_____ 13. What supplies will you need?

_____ 14. Who are your suppliers?

CUSTOMIZE THE PLAN TO MEET YOUR NEEDS

A business plan that is strictly for personal use can be short and informal. However, a business plan written to request a loan needs to be very detailed. Consider what a banker or investor needs to know about your business. Then present evidence that your plans will succeed.

No one knows all the answers when they first sit down to write a business plan. A good business plan usually requires some research. You may need to make some phone calls, go to the library, get some advice from other business people, or talk with your parents.

After you spend a lot of time writing your business plan, you won't want to shove it in a drawer somewhere and let it gather dust. Liza and LaRae keep their business plan for Lunch Box on Wheels in a portable expanding file. As the business grows and changes Liza and LaRae add new information to the appropriate file sections of their business plan.

Many young entrepreneurs like to keep their business plan on their computer, so it can be updated frequently. Whatever method you choose, remember that business planning never stops. Your business plan should be a living, breathing document that grows and changes to meet the needs of your enterprise.

1. What is your business name?

One of the best ways to let people know you are serious about your money-making plans is to give your business a name. A good business name symbolizes your business concept and tells customers what unique services or products you have to offer.

Things a business name can tell:

1. What you do (Maid-for-a-Day)
2. Who owns the business (Frankie's Crafts)
3. The location (Main Street Car Wash)
4. Quality of service   (A-OK Cookie Company)
5. Your symbol (Rainbows Unlimited)

Looking through the yellow pages of the phone book is a good way to get ideas for your name. However, you must never copy a name that is already being used by another business. Your customers will be confused, and it is usually illegal.

When you have chosen several possible names, take a survey among friends and family to see which is best received. Then practice using your new business name for a few days before you have flyers or business cards printed.

Registering an assumed name: If you plan to operate your business under any name other than your own, you must go to the office of the county clerk at the county court house and file a DBA form. DBA is short for "doing business as."

Filing a DBA form officially registers you as the owner of the business and makes it legal for you to operate under an assumed (or fictitious) name. The DBA form also reserves your business name so that no one else in the county can use it. The bank will require that you give them a copy of your DBA form if you wish to open an account in your business name. A copy of your DBA should also be included in your business plan.

2. Where is your business located?

Most young entrepreneurs do business from their home. You may need to talk to your parents about specific work areas the family is willing for you to use. Will you work in your bedroom? In the garage? In the basement? In the kitchen? In the backyard? Or do you plan to set up a booth at the local flea market? Perhaps you are starting a mobile dog-grooming business. Do you need storage space for your equipment and supplies? These are decisions that need to be made now.

Next you need to set up a place at home for an office. It doesn't have to be a large space. A corner of your bedroom or the desk where you do homework is fine. Always keep your business papers, records, and supplies in the same place.

Checklist of basic supplies for your home office:

_____ Note paper, pens, pencils

_____ 3 x 5 cards and file box

_____ Art supplies to make signs and flyers

_____ Business cards, printed or handmade

_____ Receipt book

_____ Notebook to keep records

_____ Calculator

_____ Envelopes and stationery

_____ This book

_____ Photocopies of forms from this book

_____ Your business plan

_____ Access to a phone

_____ An answering machine

3. What is the purpose of your business?

Have you ever been embarrassed when you tried to tell someone about your business because you couldn't think of the right words? The way to overcome this is to practice answering three questions: (1) Who am I? (2) What do I do? (3) What is a unique benefit (purpose) of my product or service?

When you can answer these three questions in one sentence that takes about 10 seconds to say, you will no longer feel so awkward when you meet prospective customers.

Business experts call this one-sentence, 10-second statement of concept a *mission statement*. Practice your statement on scratch paper until you are satisfied with the wording. Then copy it in your business plan.

Here are some examples of a well-planned mission statement:

> I'm Sandy Smith, owner of Morgan Street Muffin Factory, and I deliver fresh muffins to your door every Saturday morning at half the price you spend at the local market.

> I'm your neighbor, Jackie Jones, and I'm a babysitter finder, so if you need a sitter, call me first and I'll save you lots of time.

LEGAL REQUIREMENTS WORKSHEET

1. My business name is _____.
   My social security number is _____.

2. I registered my business name on (date) _____
   at the county clerk's office in _____ county.

3. The business structure I have chosen is:
   _____Sole proprietorship _____ Partnership _____Corporation

4. I called City Hall on (date) _____and spoke to
   _____about zoning, licenses, and permits.
   • Zoning laws that affect my business are:
   • Health and safety regulations I must follow are:
   • Local licenses and/or permits I need are:

5. I called the Chamber of Commerce on (date) _____
   and spoke to _____about city and state laws or
   regulations that effect my business.
   I found out I need to:_____
   _____
   _____

6. I called the state tax office on (date) _____ and spoke
   to _____about sales tax laws.
   My business needs a sales tax permit.   _____Yes   _____ No
   I have applied for my sales tax permit.   _____Yes   _____ No

7. My business will be hiring employees. _____Yes   _____ No
   I (do, do not) need a federal employer identification number.
   I applied on (date) _____ .

4. What are the legal requirements?

There are three basic legal forms of business. You must choose whether to operate your business as a sole proprietorship, a partnership, or a corporation. There are advantages and disadvantages to each.

Sole proprietorship: This is the simplest and most common form of business operation. It's easy to start and requires no legal assistance by an attorney. You are the only owner. You make all the decisions and you receive all the profits. The only disadvantage is that you have no one to share the responsibilities.

General partnership: A partnership is formed when two or more people agree to joint ownership of a business. Having partners gives you more resources, more start-up money, more workers, and (hopefully) more earnings. To avoid conflicts, partnership agreements should always be made in writing. Office supply stores have sample partnership agreements, but legal partnerships are normally set up with the help of an attorney.

Corporation: This form of business is not usually recommended for young entrepreneurs. Becoming incorporated can cost anywhere from $200 to $1,000 (or more) and usually requires an attorney to handle the paperwork.

A business that is incorporated goes by special laws. Each person who owns part of the corporation is a shareholder. Members of the corporation share the profits or the losses of the business, depending on the number of shares each owns. "Inc." is an abbreviation for the word *incorporated.* It is illegal to use this abbreviation in your business name unless you have filed legal papers to become a corporation.

Obtaining licenses and permits: When you start a business, it is very important that you obtain any licenses or permits required by your city, county, or state. A worksheet for going through these steps was shown before. Copies of your licenses and permits should be included in the business plan.

Find out what is required for your business by calling the following sources and asking for information on zoning, licenses, and permits:

City Hall (Ask for the city clerk.)

Your local homeowner's association

The Chamber of Commerce

Small Business Development Centers at local colleges

Small Business Administration offices

Other business owners in your community

Sales tax: If you are selling a product to the consumer, most states require that you collect sales tax. Service businesses, however, are usually exempt from sales tax. Since sales tax laws vary greatly, the best way to find out how to be legal is to call the state comptroller or tax assessor's office. They will tell you how to apply for a sales tax permit, how much tax to collect, and how to file your sales tax reports.

5. Who are the key people involved in your business?

Write a paragraph in your business plan about the skills, talents, and experience you are bringing into the business. Detailed information about your qualifications is particularly important if you are looking for a loan.

If your business is a partnership, include the same information about your partner. Longer biographies of each person may be attached to the back of the business plan.

Employees: Most businesses owned by young entrepreneurs do not have employees. Hiring employees requires that you have a Federal Employer Identification Number. You will also have to take care of each employee's withholding tax, and you will be required to file quarterly and yearly payroll tax returns.

Independent contractors: Rather than hiring employees, it's best to find friends to be independent contractors. When you have too much work, they "contract" to do the overflow.

For example, if you are running a year-round lawn care service, you may have too many yards to rake in the fall. Assign some of the yards to independent contractors. They pay you a portion of the money they earn on each yard because you found the jobs. So when you are out raking one yard, you may also have three independent contractors out raking three other yards. You earn 100% on the job you did and 15% on each job they did, for a total of 145% of your normal hourly rate. Arrangements like this can help you build a very profitable business.

Sales reps: Another type of independent contractor is the independent sales representative. The sales "rep" goes out looking for business, enlisting new customers, and selling your product. The sales rep receives a portion of the sales she or he makes, or a "commission" on sales.

Duties of key people: The business plan should list the duties and responsibilities of each person involved in the business. This is particularly important for avoiding disagreements in a partnership. A form to record agreements with business associates is provided on the next page.

6. How much time will you invest?

This is the time to look closely at your current schedule and determine exactly how much time you can devote to a business.

One way to get a realistic picture of your time demands is to keep a time log for 2 weeks. Each day, write down what you are doing hour by hour. Then study the log to see how you can make time to run a business and keep your customers happy. A schedule of the times you plan to work should be a part of your business plan.

Child labor laws: If your business hires other young people, you need to be aware of the child labor laws. The federal law states that anyone of age 14 or 15 can't work more than 3 hours on a school day or more than 18 hours in a school week. Kids under 14 can't work at all, unless they are employed by their parents, acting or performing, delivering newspapers, or making wreaths.

Note that these laws generally apply to hiring kids as employees, not to whether you as a young person can own a business. However, if you have further questions about the child labor laws, you should consult a lawyer or the Department of Labor.

Seasonal work: Some businesses operate only a very short time of the year. For example, a business selling Christmas trees only operates during November and December of each year. If you have a seasonal business, list the dates of the opening and closing of your business in the business plan.

Busy seasons: Some businesses that operate all year long have "busy seasons." An example might be a craft business with busy seasons at Christmas, Valentine's Day, and Mother's Day.

BUSINESS ASSOCIATE INFORMATION

Use this form to organize important information about partners, business associates, employees, independent contractors, sales representatives, or any key people in your business.

Name: _____ Phone: _____

Age: _____ Birth date: _____ Social Security No.: _____

Address: _____

City: _____ State: _____ Zip: _____

Emergency contact: _____
_____

How associated to the business: _____
_____

Financial agreements: _____
_____

Skills bringing to the business: _____
_____

Previous experience: _____
_____
_____

Duties and responsibilities in the business: _____
_____
_____

Work schedule: _____
_____

Signature: _____ Date: _____

Take time now to study the calendar year, and note the seasons you expect to be busiest with your business. Write these dates in your business plan, and tell how you plan to handle the demands on your time. A worksheet to plan your yearly busy seasons is provided on the next page.

7. What are your goals for the future?

This is the part of the business plan where you talk about the dreams you have for the future of your business. How will it grow? What will it become? Where will you be 6 months from now? A year from now? Two years from now?

Goals should be stated in terms that can be measured: How many customers do you need? What equipment will you buy? When do you expect this to happen? Give yourself a time-line for accomplishing the goal and a way to measure your success. These are some examples of goals stated in measurable terms:

> By next summer, I plan to own a riding mower and have three commercial mowing contracts.

> My next step is to find a community center where I can teach classes on how to paint T-shirts. My goal is to have six students this time and increase the attendance to ten students by the fall.

> My goal for this season's snow shoveling business is to have five kids working with me, each averaging five jobs a week at $10 a job.

Allow yourself to think big. A goal should be exciting and challenging. It should put a sparkle in your eye and make you feel like working a little harder. So give yourself a dream worth striving to achieve.

8. What are your products or services?

There are basically only two ways to earn money in the world: (1) Sell a product or (2) provide a service.

Your business may be based on selling a product like candy, T-shirts, soap, muffins, or Christmas bells. Or your business may be based on getting paid to provide a service: washing cars, shoveling snow, doing magic shows, or cleaning bird cages.

Liza and LaRae's business, Lunch Box on Wheels, is a combination of product and service. They sell food (hot dogs, tacos, candy bars, chips), and they provide the service of bringing the food to the event, setting up the tables, serving, and cleaning up.

YEARLY PLANNER

Hours I can work during school weeks:

Monday: _____

Tuesday: _____

Wednesday: _____

Thursday: _____

Friday: _____

Saturday: _____

Sunday: _____

Hours I can work when school is out:

Monday: _____

Tuesday: _____

Wednesday: _____

Thursday: _____

Friday: _____

Saturday: _____

Sunday: _____

Busiest seasons for my business:

Dates	When to Start Planning
_____	_____
_____	_____
_____	_____

Important events: (Holidays, trade shows, craft fairs, etc.)

Dates	When to Start Planning
_____	_____
_____	_____
_____	_____

Three top goals I want to reach this year:

1. _____

2. _____

3. _____

When you pay $2 a plate for their barbecue sandwiches and potato salad, you are also paying them for bringing the food where you are.

Analyze your business and make a list of the products and services you provide. Make a second list of products or services you would like to add to the business as it grows. Both of these lists are important to include in your business plan.

9. What are the advantages of your product?

The big question is: What makes your product or service better than other products available to the customer?

These are some answers Liza and LaRae might give about why their barbecue dinners are the best:

> We use high-quality beef raised right on our ranch.
>
> We don't add fillers or soy bean supplements.
>
> Our desert bars are wrapped separately so they stay fresh.
>
> We observe all health standards in food preparation.
>
> Our prices are lower than that of any other restaurant or caterer.

When you are confident your product serves your customer better, you will find it easy to sell. Spend some time writing down all the good features and advantages of your product. This list of competitive advantages will be part of your sales pitch when you start marketing. Include it in your business plan.

10. How do you produce what you sell?

Liza and LaRae have a lot of work to do when they are getting ready to cater an auction. These are some of the steps they may take:

1. Select the menu.
2. Make a shopping list.
3. Buy the supplies.
4. Gather tables and equipment.
5. Make chili the night before.
6. Bake deserts. Wrap each serving individually.
7. Ice down the cold drinks.

WORK PLANNING SHEET

Customer:_____ Phone: _____

Address: _____

City: _____ State: _____ Zip: _____

Description of work to be completed: _____

_____

Date requested: _____ Date to be completed: _____

Financial agreements: _____

_____

Equipment needed: Source:

1. _____   _____

2. _____   _____

3. _____   _____

4. _____   _____

5. _____   _____

6. _____   _____

Supplies needed: Cost:

1. _____   _____

2. _____   _____

3. _____   _____

4. _____   _____

5. _____   _____

6. _____   _____

Sales representative: _____

Person(s) who will do work: _____

Date job completed: _____ Pay received: _____

8. Pack everything into the truck.

9. Arrive early enough to set up.

10. Start making coffee.

11. Steam the hot dogs.

12. Heat the chili.

Lunch Box on Wheels is a success because Liza and LaRae plan the production of their meals in every detail. They even price everything in increments of 25 cents, so it's easy to make change, and the lines move quickly. Their plan works.

Every business needs a step-by-step plan for producing its product or service. One way to write this plan is to pretend you are trying to explain your procedures to someone who knows nothing about your business. Then write all the steps of operation in logical order and include them in your business plan.

11. How much cash are you investing?

The cash you invest to start your business is known as your *capital* investment. It's important to track how much cash you put into the business, so you know if your investment is making a profit.

Most of the businesses in this book require very little investment to get started. Service businesses are the easiest for young entrepreneurs to start because they require almost no cash outlay. Businesses that sell a product require more start-up money because you have to buy supplies to make the product, or you have to buy the product in bulk from a supplier.

If you need cash to start your business, you may have to work a service business temporarily to earn the start-up capital for the business you really want to start.

12. What equipment will be used in the business?

One of the ways to cut costs on the start-up of your business is to take equipment, machines, or tools you already own and use them to earn money. In business, this is called *converting personal assets into business assets.*

Look around your house and make a list of equipment you might use in your business. For example, if you set up an office in the corner of your bedroom, you would list your desk, lamp, chair, calculator, and phone as business assets. If your parents

INVESTMENT OF CASH AND EQUIPMENT

Cash on Hand: _____ Date: _____

BUSINESS EQUIPMENT I OWN

Item: Approximate value: Date placed in service:

1. _____ _____ _____
2. _____ _____ _____
3. _____ _____ _____
4. _____ _____ _____
5. _____ _____ _____

BUSINESS EQUIPMENT I BORROW OR RENT

Item: Rental fee: Owner:

1. _____ _____ _____
2. _____ _____ _____
3. _____ _____ _____
4. _____ _____ _____
5. _____ _____ _____

FUTURE EQUIPMENT PURCHASES NEEDED

Item: Cost: Source:

1. _____ _____ _____
2. _____ _____ _____
3. _____ _____ _____
4. _____ _____ _____
5. _____ _____ _____

give you permission to use the family lawnmower, it would be listed as one of your business assets. If you start teaching private guitar lessons, your guitar becomes a business asset.

Your business plan should include a list of all the equipment you will be using to operate your business. Indicate on the list whether you own it, borrow it, rent it, or plan to purchase it. Also list the approximate value of your equipment and the dates it was put into business use. On page 48 is a form for recording this information.

13. What supplies will you need?

Your business plan should also include a complete checklist of all the supplies you will need to operate your business. Supplies are things like the soap, wax, paper towels, and cleaning products you might need to run a car-detailing business. Or it might be the pencils, paper, and 3 x 5 cards you use to run a babysitter finder service.

Liza and LaRae's supply list for Lunch Box on Wheels includes all the ingredients for their recipes, paper plates, cups, napkins, coffee filters, coffee, hot-chocolate mix, stir stix, plastic wrap, foil, dishwashing soap, and many other items. By keeping a checklist of common supply needs, Liza and LaRae are able to watch the sales and buy supplies when prices go down. You can use this system, too.

A supply checklist also helps you save time. Before you go out to work, use your checklist to be sure you have everything you need for the job. Then you won't have to go back home and get things you forgot.

14. Who are your suppliers?

To ensure the highest rate of profit on your business, it is always important to buy your supplies at the lowest price. One way to save money is to buy in large quantities from a warehouse outlet or a wholesaler. However, it sometimes takes days or weeks of patient research to find a supplier that will give you a low enough price.

Young entrepreneurs often have additional difficulty buying at wholesale prices because the wholesalers won't accept small orders. The National Foundation for Teaching Entrepreneurship (NFTE) has published a directory of wholesalers that will accept orders of $50 or less from youth-owned businesses. To order this directory write NFTE, 64 Fulton Street, Suite 700, New York, NY 10038.

SUPPLY LIST

Office supplies (paper, pens, etc.):

Item:	Amount on hand:	Amount needed:	Unit cost:

Work supplies (soap, rags, leaf bags, etc.):

Item:	Amount on hand:	Amount needed:	Unit cost:

SUPPLY LIST

Materials to make products to sell (sugar, flour, thread, fabric, etc.):

Item:	Amount on hand:	Amount on hand:	Unit cost:
_____	_____	_____	_____
_____	_____	_____	_____
_____	_____	_____	_____
_____	_____	_____	_____
_____	_____	_____	_____
_____	_____	_____	_____
_____	_____	_____	_____
_____	_____	_____	_____
_____	_____	_____	_____
_____	_____	_____	_____

Products purchased for resale (candy, canned drinks, mugs, etc.):

Item:	Amount on hand:	Amount needed:	Unit cost:
_____	_____	_____	_____
_____	_____	_____	_____
_____	_____	_____	_____
_____	_____	_____	_____
_____	_____	_____	_____
_____	_____	_____	_____
_____	_____	_____	_____
_____	_____	_____	_____
_____	_____	_____	_____
_____	_____	_____	_____
_____	_____	_____	_____

These are some suggestions on how to form a relationship with a wholesaler:

Step 1: Call or write the wholesaler and introduce yourself. Explain that you are a youth-owned business and that you would like to make wholesale purchases. Ask about their requirements for minimum purchases and their procedures for ordering.

Step 2: Send the wholesaler your business card, a copy of your DBA form, and a copy of your resale certificate or sales tax permit. Show evidence that you are a legitimate business enterprise. Request order forms and a catalog.

Step 3: Request an appointment to visit with a customer service representative at the wholesaler's office. Dress up for the occasion, and go meet with them face to face. Take a list of what you need, and be prepared to place your first order while you're there.

Step 4: Be persistent about your desire to do business with the wholesaler. Keep calling and writing and asking for help until you get the answer you want.

Step 5: Once you find a wholesaler who will work with you, always pay your bills on time and conduct your affairs in a professional manner.

Suppliers are valuable business resources. Make a list of your suppliers' names, addresses, and phone numbers to include in your business plan.

If you have to order supplies or parts for repairs frequently, save time by keeping a list of your suppliers near your phone. You will also want to keep copies of their price lists or catalogs where you can find them easily.

As you do business with the same suppliers over a period of time, they will come to respect your business abilities and look forward to serving your requests.

NOW THAT YOU'RE ORGANIZED

If you have followed all the steps in this chapter to write a plan for organizing your new business, you are miles and miles down the road toward success. In the next chapter you will be working on a plan to get people to buy your product.

·6·

HOW TO GET CUSTOMERS

ANYONE CAN START A BUSINESS, BUT IT TAKES CUSTOMERS *TO GROW A BUSINESS.* THIS chapter is all about how to find customers, tell them about your product, and get them to buy. We call this process *marketing.*

THE MARKETING UMBRELLA

Marketing is actually an "umbrella" term that means all the things you do to tell and sell. Advertising, sales, and public relations all come under the umbrella of marketing.

When you hand out business cards or put up a sign in your yard, you are marketing. When you knock on doors and ask for jobs, you are marketing. If you give away free samples of your cookies, that's marketing. Putting an advertisement in the newspaper is marketing.

Big corporations often have whole departments of people whose only job is marketing. But most entrepreneurs start out small like you. They have no employees and they do everything themselves. They invent the business and they market the business. Once they get customers, they do all the work. (Then they get all the pay!)

Young entrepreneurs have to know how to do every job in their business. Marketing is one of the most important and creative jobs of a business owner.

ODD BALL ENTERPRISES

Jordan Levine and Josh Vinitz, seventh-graders from Bayside, New York, spend most of their time doing odd jobs. That's why they named their business Odd Ball Enterprises. In the summer they wash cars and do yards. In the fall they rake leaves. In the winter they shovel snow. In the spring they wash windows and weed flower beds. All year long they're available for running errands or delivering packages.

It takes a lot of marketing to do all that business, but Jordan and Josh don't mind. Their advertising slogan says they are willing to work: "No job too big, no job too small, so give Odd Ball a call."

When Jordan and Josh aren't doing odd jobs, they get together at Odd Ball Headquarters and plan their marketing strategies. They take surveys to find out what their customers think, give away coupons for $1 off any job, design new flyers every season, and dream of one day having a commercial on TV.

Their name, Odd Ball Enterprises, is plastered on everything they own, and they never leave home without a supply of flyers or business cards to hand out. On weekends, they go house-to-house, ringing doorbells and spreading the word about Odd Ball Enterprises.

MARKETING CAN BE FUN

How did Jordan and Josh become so enthusiastic about marketing? It started with the "odd" name they gave their business. Customers enjoyed their humor so much, that Jordan and Josh decided to try other creative ideas and slogans. Now they never seem to stop thinking of new ways to tell people about Odd Ball Enterprises.

Although they discovered it accidentally, Jordan and Josh are operating on a basic principle of success in sales: Enthusiasm is catching. The key to persuasion is to believe so much in your product that your excitement is contagious. The customer can't help but buy when you're having so much fun telling about your wonderful product!

When you enjoy what you do, it's not hard to think of all kinds of creative ways to tell people about your business.

Here are some techniques other young entrepreneurs have successfully used:

Wear your ad: Create a T-shirt advertising your business, and wear it when you go out to sell. Other items you can put your name on are caps, jackets, sweat shirts, or things you carry with you such as duffle bags, clipboards, or briefcases.

Get attention: Put balloons on your signs or streamers on your banners. Wear a costume when you sell tickets to your Halloween party. Forget the usual sales talk, and sing a rap song to sell your home-baked cookies.

Give freebies: Put coupons on your neighbors' doors for 1 hour free babysitting or a half-price car wash. Give free demonstrations of window washing. Offer free samples of your homemade candy and fudge.

Find unlikely places: Put a sign on your bike or in your car window. Ask a teacher to put your flyers in the teacher's lounge. Sell snowcones from your tailgate at the next swim meet.

Go to press: Get in your school newspaper or write an article for your community newsletter. If you're doing something unusual, call the local news reporters and invite them to attend.

CREATIVE MARKETING PAYS OFF

Smart marketing campaigns have made some entrepreneurs famous and wealthy. Estee Lauder started her career in cosmetics when she was 16, selling a skin cream manufactured by her uncle. One of her best sales strategies was to give girls at school free facials, then get them for customers. Estee Lauder believed so strongly in her products that she would stand on the sidewalk in front of dress shops and start conversations with women about caring for their skin. Whenever they bought something from her, she always gave them an additional item free.

Her first factory was a converted restaurant. Estee would sell all day and cook up her products on the old stoves at night. To overcome a limited advertising budget, she continued her policy of "free gift with purchase."

Estee's products such as Clinique, Youth Dew, and White Linen are now displayed in prestigious stores all over the world. Her earnings are reported to exceed $2 billion annually. Other companies have tried to compete against her "free gift with purchase," but Estee set the standard long ago. Those who want part of the cosmetic market today are most likely also offering "free gift with purchase."

GUIDELINES FOR WRITING THE BUSINESS PLAN
PART 2: THE MARKETING PLAN

Use this checklist as a guide for writing Part 2 of your business plan. A space has been provided for you to check off the questions as you complete the answers. All of the questions are explained in detail in the pages that follow.

A. Identify your customers.

_____ **1.** Who is your average buyer?

_____ **2.** Who are your target customers?

_____ **3.** Where is your niche in the market?

_____ **4.** How will market trends affect your business?

B. Identify the competition.

_____ **5.** Who are your main competitors?

_____ **6.** How is your product better than theirs?

_____ **7.** How can you give better service?

_____ **8.** How can you make your price competitive?

C. Plan your marketing methods.

_____ **9.** What market tests will help you make decisions?

_____ **10.** What advertising methods are best for you?

_____ **11.** What sales literature do you need?

_____ **12.** What will you say when you go out to sell?

_____ **13.** How can you use public relations to get customers?

_____ **14.** What is your marketing timetable?

MARKETING GENIUS AT WORK

Soichiro Honda changed the motorcycle industry more than any other person in the world when he introduced his marketing campaign "You Meet the Nicest People on a Honda" in the late 1960s. Until that time, the image of a biker was black leather jackets, boots, and chains. Honda was the first to build unisex bikes with step-through mounts. His upbeat marketing slogans made motorcycles and dirtbikes socially acceptable as good family fun by the 1970s.

Ben Cohen and Jerry Greenfield started Ben & Jerry's Ice Cream in 1978 after completing a $5 correspondence course from Penn State University on how to make ice cream. Good friends since seventh grade, their unofficial motto was "If it's not fun, why do it?" They marketed their product by giving away free ice cream and sponsoring local festivals. Their "Save the Rain Forest" campaigns have made them two of America's favorite business people. Today Ben & Jerry's annual sales are over $100 million.

PLANNING YOUR CAMPAIGN

In the last chapter, you spent a lot of time writing Part 1 of your business plan and defining the organizational structure of your business. In this chapter, you will use your imagination and creativity to write Part 2: The Marketing Plan.

On page 56 you will find the guidelines for writing your marketing plan. Notice that the outline covers three basic components of marketing: the customer, the competition, and your marketing methods. These brief terms outline three important steps you will take.

THREE STEPS TO SUCCESSFUL MARKETING

1. *Think like your customer.* Where do your customers live? Where do they shop? Do they have kids? Pets? A pool? What do customers expect from your product? What do they need? The more you understand the needs of your customers, the more likely you are to make a sale.

2. *Use competition to make you better.* Competition inspires entrepreneurs to work harder and be sharper. Instead of being afraid of competition, welcome the challenge.

SURVEY
WHO NEEDS MY PRODUCT OR SERVICE?

What age group does my product appeal to? _____

My customers are primarily: _____ male _____ female

My customers are: _____ married _____ single _____ students

They are: _____ professionals _____ homemakers _____ retired _____ business owners _____ factory workers

Other occupations may be _____

Do they have children? _____ If so, what ages?_____

Do they have pets?_____ If so, what kinds?_____

They live in: _____ a suburban neighborhood _____ rural area _____ semirural area _____ a small town _____ a large city

Do they: _____ own a home? _____ live in an apartment? _____ rent a home? _____ live on a farm?

Hobbies my customers are likely to have: _____

_____

Clubs or groups my customers belong to: _____

_____

Other facts I know about my customers: _____

_____

After answering these questions, use the space below and a separate sheet of paper to write a brief description of your average customer.

3. *Prepare a plan to promote your product.* Good marketing is never haphazard. The right product must be presented to the right people, at the right price, at the right place, with the right promotion. All this takes planning.

1. Who is your average buyer?

Big business spends lots of time and money knowing about the people who buy their products. For example, they often conduct demographic surveys that provide facts and statistics (age, income, occupation, etc.) about their typical customers. When they know more about their customers, they know how to sell more products.

You can use this system, too. The survey sheet on page 58 asks demographic questions that help describe your typical customer. After you have answered the questions, write a description of the average customer who needs your product, and include it in your business plan.

Best customers: If you have been in business for a while, you may already have some "best" customers. They are people who almost always say Yes. You wish you had a hundred customers like them. Use the questions on the survey to study your best customers. Then use what you learn to find more people like them.

2. Who are your target customers?

Young entrepreneurs often dread going out to sell because they fear being told No. However, it isn't realistic to expect everyone to say Yes. In fact, experts tell us most salespeople have to make ten calls to get one Yes.

There is a way to cut down on the number of No's you hear. Find the people who need your product most and ask them first. These "target customers" are more likely to say Yes.

Jordan and Josh, owners of Odd Ball Enterprises, have learned who are their best customers. Jordan says his mom goes to their synagogue and talks to all the "older ladies who are widows." They are Jordan and Josh's favorite customers because "they appreciate your work, they always pay you right away, and sometimes they give you cookies."

WHO ARE MY TARGET CUSTOMERS?

1. List four groups of people who are target markets for your business. (Examples: dog owners, mothers of small children, senior adults, kids who like music)

Target markets: Where to find them:

_____   _____

_____   _____

_____   _____

_____   _____

_____   _____

2. Number the target markets according to their rank of importance to your business.

3. Beside each, write the main place you might find these groups of people. (Examples: PTA meetings, pet shops, tennis courts, school, church, etc.)

4. List names of target customers you already know (friends, relatives, former customers, etc.).

   1. _____   7. _____

   2. _____   8. _____

   3. _____   9. _____

   4. _____   10. _____

   5. _____   11. _____

   6. _____   12. _____

5. Start a card file on target customers. At the top of each card write the customer's name, address, and phone number. Then make notes about pets, children, hobbies, what they last bought from you, favorite colors, and special requests. Each time you contact the customer write down the date, result, and when you should contact them again.

The answers on your demographic survey may have shown several groups of target customers. Some are primary or "top priority" customers. But there may be second or third groups who are almost as important to your business. Use the worksheet on page 60 to rate your target markets, and begin making a list of the target customers you already know.

3. Where is your niche in the market?

Small-business owners are able to do something most large companies can't afford to do. The small-business person can serve the needs of very small groups of people and still make a profit. For example, big business would lose a lot of money marketing only to older Jewish widows in Bayside, New York. But Jordan and Josh make their greatest profit serving nice Jewish grandmothers in Bayside.

Marketing to a very small, specific group of people who you know very well is called *niche marketing*. Niche markets to consider are your scout troop, 4-H group, school friends, church friends, relatives, or parents' co-workers. These small, intimate groups of people often become your most loyal and profitable customers.

Spend some time identifying niche markets where you can serve the customer better than a large company. What products or services do you have to offer these small groups of people? How can you make their lives better? How will you reach them? Include the answers to these questions in your business plan.

4. How will market trends affect your business?

The market never stays the same. Just about the time you think you have defined your market and learned how to reach your customers, be assured something will change. Sometimes change is positive and exciting and increases your business. Sometimes it means you lose money.

Suppose you were in the candy-selling business like Cathryn Murray in Chapter 1. Imagine how these changes in the market would affect your income:

1. You have been selling candy at school during class breaks. The teachers become annoyed because so many kids are eating candy in class, and the principal makes a rule that there will be no more selling candy on school property.

SURVEY: WHO IS MY COMPETITOR?

Fill out one of these survey forms for each of your competitors. Update the information on each competitor frequently and include these forms in your business plan.

Competitor's business name: _____

Owner's name: _____

Location of business: _____

_____

Phone: _____   Phone: _____

List services/products offered: Prices:

_____   _____

_____   _____

_____   _____

_____   _____

_____   _____

_____   _____

Equipment my competitor uses: _____

_____

_____

Main method of advertising: _____

_____

_____

Ways our businesses are alike: _____

_____

Ways our businesses are different: _____

_____

2. Another kid on your block sees how much money you're making selling candy in the neighborhood and decides to sell candy, too. He sets his prices a little lower and starts taking some of your best customers.

3. A wealthy family with five kids who all get big allowances and love candy moves in next door to you.

Smart entrepreneurs plan ahead for changes in the market that might affect their business. One market trend that is really boosting business for young entrepreneurs is the increase in demand for service businesses. As more families become two-income, there is more demand for lawn care services, babysitting services, and cleaning services of all kinds.

Staying informed: Sometimes being aware of market trends is as simple as listening to what the kids say at school or to your parents' conversation at the dinner table. You can also read the newspaper, listen to news on TV, read magazines, and pay attention to political events. Some of your best research will be talking to your customers and noting their needs and concerns.

Take time to think of market changes that could affect the future of your business. Include this information in your business plan.

5. Who are your main competitors?

Instead of being mad or worried about your competition, you should call all your competitors and tell them thanks. Here's why. Competitors make us work harder and get better at our jobs. They force us to dig a little deeper, reach a little higher, be more creative, and become more skilled at serving our customers.

Competitors are an excellent source of research material. By watching your competitors, you can learn more about your market, get ideas for promotions, set prices, and avoid making costly mistakes.

If you can learn all this from competitors, isn't it time you really studied your competition closely? Here's how to find your competitors:

Look in the yellow pages of the phone book.

Read ads in local newspapers.

Watch for signs as you drive through your neighborhood.

Call the Chamber of Commerce and ask who provides
the same product or service as you.

Use the survey form on page 62 to learn everything you can about your competitors. If possible, visit your competitor's business, and pick up copies of flyers, business cards, and sales materials. Cut their ads out of the paper and study them. Buy samples of their products and see how they compare to yours.

On the back of each survey, write notes about what you learned, and attach your competitor's sales materials. Include all of this information in your business plan.

6. How is your product better than theirs?

In Chapter 1, Cathryn Murray had some advice for young people who want to start a business. She said, "Find a need and fill it."

Now you will learn another principle that goes along with that: Find a need and fill it *better than your competitor*. If you can do a better job satisfying the customer's needs, you will outsell your competitor.

Psychologists say people buy to satisfy emotional needs (feelings) and rational needs (thinking). If you want to satisfy customers' emotional needs, you help them look better, feel better, be happier, and have more fun. If you want to satisfy customers' rational needs, you give them products that are low in cost, efficient, last a long time, and get lots of work done.

What needs does your product or service satisfy? Mark your answers on the checklist below.

Buying decisions based on feelings:

_____ Feels good

_____ Looks good

_____ More fun

_____ Pride of ownership

_____ To be part of the crowd

_____ Increases self-esteem

_____ Other _____

Buying decisions based on thinking:

_____ Durability of product

_____ Lower price

_____ Higher efficiency

_____ Better performance

_____ Dependability

_____ Special features

_____ Other _____

After you have analyzed what needs your product satisfies for your customer, you will have a very good idea why your product is better. Make a list of all the ways your product is better and include it in the business plan.

7. How can you give better service?

No matter what product you sell, there is always one way you can beat your competition: Give better service.

Better service doesn't cost you anything to perform, but it often spells the difference between making or losing a sale. For example, whom would you rather pay $20 to mow your yard? Some kid who hates to mow yards, but does the job to earn a buck, or an enthusiastic young entrepreneur who does something extra and smiles and says Thanks! when he gets paid? When given a choice, customers will always vote for the person who is friendly and enthusiastic.

Here is a checklist of ways young entrepreneurs can beat their competition by giving better service:

_____ Be friendlier.

_____ Be faster.

_____ Be more polite.

_____ Answer phone calls sooner.

_____ Give more time.

_____ Show more effort.

_____ Know more about the customer.

SERVICE GUARANTEE

Description of job: _____

_____

Description of product: _____

_____

Standards guaranteed:

   1. _____

   2. _____

   3. _____

   4. _____

   5. _____

   6. _____

   7. _____

   8. _____

Time limit on guarantee: _____

_____

If customer is not satisfied I guarantee to: _____

_____

_____

Refund policy: _____

_____

Signed: _____

Business: _____

Date: _____

_____ Know more about the product.

_____ Anticipate the customer's needs.

_____ Offer a warranty or guarantee.

_____ Really care.

Keep a card file on your regular customers with notes about what they buy, color preferences, birth dates, children's names and ages, pet's names, special requests, important instructions, emergency numbers—any information that will help you provide better service in the future.

On page 66 you will find a sample service guarantee to offer your customers. It is a good idea to decide your standards of quality and set your policy for refunds when you are writing your business plan. Don't wait until you are standing in front of the customer to fill this out. These policies take thought and planning.

The secret to good customer service is a genuine spirit of caring. Treat all people you meet as if they are the most important customers you have that day. (At that moment, they are!) Give more than the customers expect—more time, more effort, more service —and they won't ever forget you.

8. How can you make your price competitive?

There are two basic approaches to price setting that every young entrepreneur needs to understand. The approach you choose depends on the type of product you sell. Are you selling a service or are you selling merchandise?

If you are selling services such as window washing, pool cleaning, and closet organizing, your prices are mostly based on charges for labor. Your main goal is to match or outbid the average rate your competitors charge for the same service. The information you collected in the survey of your competitors earlier in the chapter well help you.

If you are selling merchandise of any kind, you must carefully consider your costs before you set a price. The National Foundation for Teaching Entrepreneurship (NFTE) teaches young entrepreneurs to understand how a product travels from the manufacturer to the consumer and how the cost increases along the way. NFTE calls this the *production structure of business*. These are the steps in the production process:

1. Manufacturer: Uses raw materials to make the product
2. Wholesaler: Distributes the product to the stores
3. Retailer: The store where the consumer shops
4. Consumer: The end-user of the product

The important factor to remember is that the price of the product nearly doubles at each level of the production process. For example, it may cost about $1 to manufacture a basket in a basket factory. To make a profit, the basket manufacturer doubles its cost and sells the basket to the wholesaler at $2. The wholesaler has to make a profit, too. It doubles the price and sells the basket to the retailer for $4. The retailer then doubles the wholesale price and puts the basket on display in the store. The final price the consumer pays is $8.

If you are in the business of making gift baskets, you can't beat your competitor's price if you are buying baskets from the retailer at $8 each. NFTE teaches young entrepreneurs to go back up the line of production, skip the retailer, and buy from the wholesaler at $4 or even from the manufacturer at $2. When you are able to cut your costs, you can pass the savings along to your customer and beat the competition.

9. What market tests will help you make decisions?

When Cathryn Murray had the idea that kids in her Pittsburgh neighborhood would buy candy, she needed a way to see if her plan would work. To cut down on risk, she used her leftover Halloween candy to test the market. Once she found out kids would buy candy, she invested money in the business.

Jordan and Josh, owners of Odd Ball Enterprises, conduct market tests also. They hand out surveys that say, "We care about what you think of us!" On the surveys are questions about their prices, their service, and whether the customer would hire them to do additional work.

Big business spends a lot of money on market tests before a new product is released. It tests the color, packaging, prices, size, smell, texture—all aspects of the product. Big companies save money by knowing what will sell before they manufacture and mass-market their product.

Most testing methods used by young entrepreneurs are low-cost and simple. Here are some ways you might test before starting a cookie-baking service:

Take a survey of prospective customers asking what are their favorite cookies, where they buy them, and how much they pay.

Make a list of six different cookies you can bake and ask friends and neighbors to vote for their favorites.

Set up a table at your next scout, 4-H, or youth meeting, and offer a choice of bar cookies, drop cookies, or rolled cookies. See which variety is most popular with the youth market.

Make a list of ways you can test the market and make better business decisions. On page 70 is a form for taking market surveys about your product or service. Each time you conduct a market test, the results should be used to update your business plan.

10. What advertising methods are best for you?

Paid advertising is not generally a good way for young entrepreneurs to build a business. It takes many weeks of repeating the same ad again and again in the paper before you start getting significant response. Another drawback of paid advertising is that it covers a much larger area than you are most likely prepared to service. Don't waste your money by advertising too far away from home unless you have reliable transportation.

Talking to customers person-to-person is the best way to get a job or sell your product. However, there are other ways to get jobs.

1. *Work for your parents.* Most young entrepreneurs start out this way. Parents are the main employers of kids.

2. *Get other people to spread the word.* Your parents or other family members can help by telling co-workers, neighbors, or relatives about your business.

3. *Get a partner.* Young entrepreneurs who are shy about talking to customers find it easier with a friend along for moral support. Working with friends can be more fun, too.

4. *Get customers to call you first.* Announce your business to the community with flyers, cards, and signs. You won't hear a lot of No's because only the customers who are really interested will call.

PRODUCT SURVEY

Dear Customers, Neighbors, and Friends:

We care what you think about our business. So we are using this survey to ask your opinion about the following product:

Product: _____

Description: _____

Price: _____

You can help us greatly by taking a few minutes to answer the questions below. Your answers will help us serve you better. Thank you!

1. Would you use this product or service? _____ Yes _____ No

2. Why or why not?_____

   _____

3. How often would you use it? _____

   _____

4. What features do you like about it? _____

   _____

5. What ways can we improve it?_____

   _____

6. How do you feel about the price?_____
   _____ Too low _____ Too high _____ About right

7. What similar product or service do you now use? _____

   _____

8. How much do you now pay? _____

   _____

The good news is that advertising a youth-owned business doesn't have to be expensive. In fact, the best advertising in the world is free: word-of-mouth advertising. When your happy customers tell others about your good service, your business will grow. No paid advertising can do what word-of-mouth advertising does for a business.

Referrals: Practice looking for opportunities for word-of-mouth advertising. When a customer is pleased with your work, ask if he or she has any friends who need a similar product or service. These referrals are your hottest business leads. Follow up on them immediately, or ask your customer to call and introduce you to the friend.

Networking: Another way to get word-of-mouth advertising is known in the business world as *networking.* Networking is friends helping friends. Watch for ways to help your friends build their business, and they will soon start looking for ways to help you build your business. Working together, you can all reach your goals faster.

Whatever methods you choose, your goal should be to get the word about your business to as many people as possible in as many different ways as possible. The more times prospective customers hear or see your name, the more likely they will be to call when they need your service.

On page 72 is an advertising checklist you can use to create a master plan for advertising your business. This is a form you will want to use again and again as your business grows and the market changes.

11. What sales literature do you need?

There are three basic tools of low-cost advertising that almost every young entrepreneur uses to get started:

1. *Flyers:* An artfully designed flyer is the number-one best way of advertising. These one-sheet advertisements can be given to customers, left on front doors, and placed on bulletin boards all over your community. Flyers with coupon offers usually get the most results.

2. *Business* cards: Cards are mini-advertisements you can take anywhere you go. You can make your own or spend about $20 to have 1,000 printed at a copy shop. Cards make you look and feel more professional. They can be tacked up almost anywhere or handed directly to business contacts.

ADVERTISING CHECKLIST

Use this checklist to plan the methods of advertising you will use to promote your business.

_____ Yard signs (Where? _____)

_____ Banners/posters (Where? _____)

_____ Flyers (Where? _____)

_____ Bulletin boards (Where? _____)

_____ Business cards   _____ Door-to-door selling

_____ Brochures   _____ Surveys

_____ Backgrounder   _____ Phone calls

_____ Referral from customer   _____ Referral by family

_____ Things to wear: _____ Mailings:

    _____ T-shirts   _____ Birthdays

    _____ Caps   _____ Thank-you notes

    Other: _____   _____ Reminder notes

_____ Attention getters: _____ Freebies:

    _____ Buttons   _____ Coupons

    _____ Balloons   _____ Samples

    _____ Costume   _____ Demonstrations

    _____ Advertising slogan   _____ ½ Price offer

    Other: _____   Other: _____

_____ In the news: _____ Unusual places:

    _____ School paper   _____ Car window

    _____ Local newsletters   _____ Sign on bike

    _____ Newspaper/shopper   Other: _____

3. *Signs:* Yard signs, banners, and posters are most effective where you have big spaces to advertise. They are excellent for big jobs like garage sales, yard work, washing cars, firewood for sale, and pool cleaning.

Before you spend money on supplies to make signs or flyers, look around your house. Use leftover school supplies, art supplies, poster paints, ink markers, colored paper, index cards, and anything else you find to make inexpensive advertising pieces. Customers will appreciate your creativity and imagination.

Here are some other tips to save money on advertising materials:

Use your computer to design and print flyers, banners, business cards, postcards, surveys, and letters.

Compare prices on printing and photocopying. Cost per page can vary from 3 cents each to 15 cents each.

Instead of ordering expensive letterheads and envelopes, use inexpensive return address labels to personalize your correspondence. You can usually order these from magazine or newspaper ads for about $4 per 500.

Additional advertising materials: In addition to the standard business cards and flyers, there are a number of other advertising pieces you may find useful:

1. *Brochures:* These one-sheet advertising pieces are helpful when you need to tell more information than fits on a flyer. The advertising message is written in paragraphs, lists, and columns on both sides of the paper and triple-folded like a small booklet.

2. *Price lists:* These can be printed separately as one-sheet or half-sheet handouts. A price list makes it much easier to be firm about your prices with customers.

3. *Backgrounders:* Telling others about your skills and experience is a necessary part of sales. If you don't like talking about yourself, type up a list of facts about who you are and why you are qualified to run your business. This is called a *backgrounder.*

SALES SCRIPT WORKSHEET

Use this worksheet to write and practice your basic sales presentation.

1. Start with a simple introduction. (Your mission statement is ideal. Tell who you are, what you do, and the purpose of your business.)

   _____

   _____

2. Briefly describe your product:
   (Explain what it is, how it works, unique features, colors, etc.)

   _____

   _____

3. Talk about the benefits of the product: (People want to buy products that solve problems, improve life, make work easier, save time, make them beautiful, etc.)

   _____

   _____

4. Use a statement that asks people to buy now: (Example: Would you prefer to order one or take advantage of our special price on three?)

   _____

   _____

5. Plan what to do if they say No: (Think of possible objections a customer might have and how you can answer each. If they still say No, ask if they have a friend who needs the product.)

   _____

   _____

6. Plan what to do if they say Yes:
   (Get their signatures on order forms and deliver what you promised.)

   _____

   _____

4. *Testimonials:* When customers say good things about your work, ask them to write a short letter stating why they enjoyed doing business with you. Copies of these letters are great handouts when you talk to new customers.

5. *Product literature:* Sometimes the suppliers or manufacturers where you buy your products for resale provide sales literature. These pieces make a great addition to your arsenal of sales materials.

Remember that people like to do business with people they trust. Good sales literature gives information that builds trust. It is your most important marketing tool. Attach copies of all your sales literature to your business plan.

12. What will you say when you go out to sell?

On page 74 you will find a worksheet that explains how to plan a simple sales presentation. Use the worksheet to prepare a sales talk, then practice it in front of a mirror until you feel comfortable.

You probably won't say the exact words you practiced when you go out to sell. But if you forget what to do next, you can always fall back on your memorized speech.

Anyone can improve as a salesperson with study and practice. Bookstores and libraries have huge sections of books on sales. If you enjoy sales, you will enjoy studying the art of salesmanship.

These are some of the keys to effective sales for young entrepreneurs:

1. *Attitude:* Successful salespeople today see themselves as partners with the customer. Your job is to find the customers who need help solving a problem, and show them how you can be of service. An attitude like this gives you confidence and purpose.

2. *Contact:* The sales process starts with your first eye contact with the customer. So greet customers warmly, smile, shake hands, and look them in the eye.

3. *Find the buyer's need:* Ask information-gathering questions that allow customers to tell you what they need or want. Determine how your product can solve their problems.

ORDER FORM

Business name: _____

Address: _____

Phone: _____

Customer's name: _____

Customer address: _____

City: _____ State: _____ Zip: _____

Phone: _____ Phone: _____

Product Ordered: Quantity: Price:

1. _____   _____   _____

2. _____   _____   _____

3. _____   _____   _____

4. _____   _____   _____

5. _____   _____   _____

6. _____   _____   _____

Special instructions: _____

_____

_____

Service to be performed: _____

_____

Price: _____ Date to be completed: _____

Sales representative: _____

Customer's signature: _____

Date: _____

4. *Establish value:* Show your customer some ways you can help. This establishes your service as valuable.

5. *Answer objections:* Respect your customer's intelligence. Answer questions with facts and evidence.

6. *Ask for the sale:* Many sales are lost because the sales person never really asks for the sale. Ask for the sale with a question that can't be answered with Yes or No. Example: If there are no more questions, when is a good time for me to meet with you to plan Susie's party?

7. *Stop talking:* After you ask for the sale, be quiet and let the customer answer. If you keep talking, the customer never has a chance to reply.

8. *Get their signature:* Carry an order form (like the one on page 76) or a sign-up sheet with you when you go out to sell. It's easy to ask for the sale by saying, "If you'll just sign this order form, I'll deliver your cookies on Saturday." Signing the form closes the sale and gives you a written record to be sure you fill the order correctly.

13. How can you use public relations to get customers?

Public relations is another umbrella term (like *marketing*) that means anything you do to build goodwill between you and your customers. Goodwill almost always results in sales, sooner or later.

In one sense, every contact you have with a potential customer is public relations. However, when writing a marketing plan, public relations means specific actions, events, or programs that build customer relations.

These are some successful public relations strategies for young entrepreneurs:

1. *Volunteer on a committee:* Volunteering is a great way to demonstrate your skills and prove you can be dependable. *Examples:* To promote your desktop-publishing business, you could volunteer to design flyers for a church or civic group. To show off your skills in lawn care, volunteer on a committee that's redoing the landscaping at your school or public library.

2. *Cosponsor an event:* Go together with other young entrepreneurs to sponsor a dinner for the homeless, a fall festival, a contest, or a trade

show. *Example:* Students at Alva Middle School in Alva, Oklahoma, in vocational technology and science classes worked together to put on a schoolwide trade show. Any student with a business or a new invention could have a table to sell products or conduct market surveys.

3. *Donate to a cause:* Almost every organization or business has a favorite charity. Offer to donate a percentage of your sales to their charity if you can have a table and sell at one of its meetings. *Examples:* Sell candy at the PTA meeting and donate 20% to the school library for books. Have a Christmas gift-wrapping service at a local gift shop, and donate 10% to feed the homeless.

4. *Provide a door prize:* Get the name of your business announced at a club meeting or school event by providing a door prize. *Example:* If you make gift baskets, donate a basket filled with chocolates and hearts for a door prize at the next Valentine's dance. *Hint:* Put your gift on display during the event, and be sure to provide a 3 x 5 card with the exact wording you want read by the announcer.

5. *Speak for free:* Offer to speak, give a class, or put on free demonstrations of your skills. *Example:* Inform the public about your puppet shows for birthday parties by giving a free puppet show at the public library.

6. *Send in your news:* Getting your story in the newspaper is better than an ad, because readers pay more attention to stories than ads. When something newsworthy happens in your business, write up a short announcement or article and send it with a picture to your local newspapers and community newsletters. *Examples:* Send in stories about the opening of your new business or your free puppet show at the library.

When you do volunteer work, be sure to wear a brightly colored T-shirt with the name of your business and your marketing slogan on the front and back. Hand out business cards to people you meet on committees or work crews. Make friends with people in the community and sales will come naturally as a result.

14. What is your marketing timetable?

The last item that goes in Part 2: The Marketing Plan is a time-line of your marketing goals.

Goals for start-up: You can't do all the steps outlined in this chapter at once. So make a step-by-step list of what you must do to put your marketing plan into action. Then give yourself a week-by-week time-line for accomplishing your goals until the business is through the start-up stage.

Long-range goals: Growing a business also requires a vision of where you want to be 2 or 3 years from now. Read this chapter again, review your business plan, and set marketing goals for the next 6 months, 12 months, 18 months, and further. Don't worry if you're not sure how you'll reach the goals right now. As you get more experience, you'll know what to do next.

YOU'RE ON THE MOVE

Now that your marketing plan is in place, something exciting is about to happen. Your business is going to grow. And you are going to have decisions to make about money. The next chapter will help you plan effective ways to handle your finances.

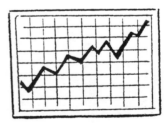

NOTES

·7·

How to Handle the Money You Make

LARRY VILLELLA LOVES A GOOD DEBATE. IN FEBRUARY 1993, JUST AFTER BILL CLINTON took office as President of the United States, Larry was watching TV in his Fargo, North Dakota, home. Larry, age 14 at the time, was doing research for a speech about the national economy. He figured watching the congressional debates on TV might give him some good ideas to win speech contests.

As he watched Congress members debate about ways to reduce America's federal debt, it seemed ridiculous to Larry that all they did was argue. It didn't appear that Congress would pass any legislation to solve this problem for many months to come. That bothered Larry a lot.

Over the weekend, Larry thought more and more about the federal deficit. He felt the American people needed to send a strong message to Congress demanding less talk and more action. That's when Larry made a decision to do something that amazed and influenced people all over the United States in the days and weeks that followed.

That Sunday afternoon, Larry sat down and wrote President Clinton a letter and a check for $1,000 to help pay the federal deficit. Larry didn't know if his plan would work, but he hoped his donation would inspire a grass roots movement among the American people to solve the problem of the federal debt.

WHERE DID LARRY VILLELLA GET ALL THAT MONEY?

When Larry was 11 years old, his most-hated chore was watering the shrubs and trees in his front yard. It was a long, slow process that required watching the clock and moving the hose to a different spot every 10 to 15 minutes. Larry thought it was a complete waste of time. So he invented a watering system that made the job easier.

His invention, the ConServ Sprinkler, is a flexible watering ring that encircles the base of a small tree or shrub, making it possible to water all sides at once. It has an adjustable water regulator and sprinkler holes on both top and bottom to moisten the ground evenly and save water.

The first model, constructed when Larry was in sixth grade, was adapted from an old circular sprinkler he found around the house. That year, Larry's ConServ Sprinkler won grand prize in his school's Invent America competition. One of the judges advised Larry to find a way to manufacture and market the new product.

A few months later, with the support of his parents and guidance from Fargo's Service Corp of Retired Executives (SCORE), Larry started his own business, ConServ Products Company. The family set up a work area in the basement and took turns helping in the manufacturing process. Local businesses provided space in their stores to sell the sprinklers.

To get people to go to the stores and buy the sprinklers, Larry sent press releases and free samples of the sprinkler to all the local newspapers, radio, and TV stations. Everyone loved the story of the local boy inventor. Sales started slowly, averaging about 1,000 sprinklers a year the first 3 years. Then Wal-Mart and K-Mart agreed to stock the ConServ Sprinkler, and sales jumped to an average of 20,000 a year.

Since 1992, Larry's business has brought in a gross income of over $115,000. That's how Larry Villella, a 14-year-old high school student from Fargo, North Dakota, was able to write President Clinton a check for $1,000 to help pay off the national debt.

WHAT HAPPENED TO THE $1,000 CHECK?

On Monday morning, Larry sent the check and the letter to President Clinton by overnight Federal Express delivery. To be sure Congress also got the message, Larry needed a little help from the media. He faxed a copy of his letter to the *Minneapolis Tribune.* By noon on Monday, reporters and newscasters all across the nation were calling Fargo asking to talk to Larry. At 1 PM, Larry's parents got him out of school so he could come home and meet the reporters gathering in front of their house.

Larry, a rather serious young man, never intended to cause that much uproar over his actions. Reporters and camera crews rang the front doorbell every 30 minutes. The four phone lines in the house rang constantly. At least three talk shows in New York wanted Larry to fly there the next day. Numerous radio stations called for on-the-spot phone interviews.

Finally around 4 PM, a call came from the White House. President Clinton hadn't received Larry's check yet, but he had heard about Larry on the news. The spokesperson said the President would be calling Larry within the next hour. More reporters began to arrive at his house. There was a frenzy of activity as the press set up cameras and mikes to tape Larry's conversation with Clinton.

When the President called, he thanked Larry for his donation and told Larry he was "a symbol of what's best with this country." President Clinton said he wasn't sure the government could accept the money, and he would let Larry know what they were going to do with the check.

The next day, Larry spent the morning doing local TV appearances, then flew to New York to appear on the *Phil Donohue Show*. In a few weeks, Larry received a personal letter from President Clinton, returning his check and advising him to send the money to a special government fund called Fund for Reducing the Public Debt.

Larry reports that right after he made his contribution, overall donations to this fund doubled. He was satisfied he had accomplished his goal.

What many people don't know is that Larry also promised future donations to the fund, based on sales of his ConServ Sprinklers. The second year, Larry sent the President another check for $750, a donation of 5 cents for every sprinkler he sold in 1993.

WHY DIDN'T HE JUST SEND $20?

Some people who heard the story of Larry's $1,000 donation to the federal deficit said, "Why didn't he just send $20?" After all, it took hours and hours of hard work to manufacture all those sprinklers and make all those sales.

Larry thought about it a long time before he chose to send $1,000. He knew he was giving away money he had worked hard to earn. But he knew $20—or even $100—

wasn't enough to make a statement to the people of the United States. It had to be a large enough amount to be a real sacrifice, or it wouldn't mean anything.

Because his business was well organized and he had kept good records, Larry knew he could afford to write a check to help with the federal deficit. He talked it over with his parents, and they agreed he should follow his convictions.

THE TRUE WORTH OF MONEY

A long time ago, a Greek slave named Aesop told a story about a man who loved money. This man was a *miser,* someone who hoards money and property but never uses any of it.

The old miser was worried that he might somehow lose his property. So he sold everything and bought one huge lump of gold. He hid the gold but went to visit it every day to be sure his treasure was still safe.

His fellow workmen became curious. Suspecting there was a treasure, they followed him one day. As soon as the old miser went home, the workmen stole the lump of gold. When the miser returned and found that he had been robbed, he wept loudly and pulled his hair.

A neighbor heard the miser crying and asked what had happened. Then the wise neighbor said, "Don't worry about it any more. Just take a stone and put it in the place where you kept your gold. You never meant to use it, so the one will do you as much good as the other."

Aesop told this story because he wanted to say something important about money. Having money is nice. But what you do with the money to help yourself and others determines the true value of your wealth.

What do you plan to do with the money you make? Will you buy things you need? Will you save for college? Will you help people less fortunate than you? Will you reinvest your money to make more money?

Larry Villella showed what he valued by the way he chose to spend his money. As you read this chapter and make decisions about how to handle your money, remember the words of Aesop: "The worth of money is not in its possession, but in its use."

PLANNING YOUR FINANCIAL STRATEGY

Chapters 5 and 6 helped you organize your business and plan ways to market your product. In this chapter, you will complete Part 3 of your business plan: The Financial Plan.

On page 86 you will find the guidelines for writing the financial plan. This outline shows three basic elements of money management for young entrepreneurs:

1. *The expenses:* Know how much you're investing.

2. *The income:* Know how much you're earning.

3. *Record keeping:* Make sure you have good cash flow.

If you are applying for a loan or trying to enlist investors, a fourth section has been included to help you write a loan request.

THE MARKS OF A REAL BUSINESS

Starting a business is exciting. It's easy for young entrepreneurs to get caught up in the thrill of starting a business, creating products, designing flyers, meeting customers, and filling orders. Sometimes it's so much fun you don't stop to keep any records or to see whether you're really making a profit for all the time you're investing.

That's why it's important to have a financial plan and a record-keeping system right from the beginning. These are some of the things good business records tell you:

How much profit you're making

What bills you need to pay

Who owes you money

Whether you're charging enough

How you might cut expenses

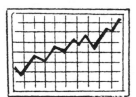

Whether you can afford new equipment

How much tax you owe

Whether you can spend any money on yourself

How much money you can donate to charity

GUIDELINES FOR WRITING THE BUSINESS PLAN
PART 3: THE FINANCIAL PLAN

Use this checklist as a guide for writing Part 3 of your business plan. A space has been provided to check off the questions as you complete the answers. All of the questions are explained in detail in the pages that follow.

A. Calculate your expenses:

_____ 1. How much money do you need to start the business?

_____ 2. Where can you get start-up money?

_____ 3. What are your monthly operating expenses?

_____ 4. What is your cost of goods?

B. Estimate your income:

_____ 5. What is your selling price?

_____ 6. How much do you have to sell to break even?

_____ 7. What are your sales goals?

C. Set up a record-keeping system:

_____ 8. How will you set up a bookkeeping system?

_____ 9. What business forms do you need?

_____ 10. What bank do you plan to use?

_____ 11. How will you maintain a positive cash flow?

D. The loan request:

_____ 12. How much money do you need to borrow?

_____ 13. How do you plan to use the money you borrow?

_____ 14. How will you repay the loan?

_____ 15. What can you offer as collateral?

_____ 16. What is your evidence of financial responsibility?

Good record keeping will be emphasized throughout this chapter. It is the mark of a real business enterprise that's run by a professional young entrepreneur.

1. How much money do you need to start the business?

Now is the time to sit down with a pencil and paper and get serious about the financial end of your business. Before you invest your time and money, you want to know if it's going to be profitable. The first step is to consider the start-up costs.

Earlier in the business plan, you created several lists that will now be helpful:

List of equipment

List of supplies

List of steps of operation or production

Lists of ways you plan to advertise

Go over these lists carefully, and write down everything you'll need to start the business. Beside each item, write an estimated cost.

Some examples of start-up costs are: flyers, business cards, signs, equipment to mow yards, supplies to bake cookies, a computer, bookkeeping software, a telephone, answering machine, and special safety clothing or a uniform.

Since most young entrepreneurs have very little money to invest, keeping start-up costs down is important. These are some ways to save money on your start-up:

1. *Borrow or rent equipment for the first few jobs.* Example: Most kids start out borrowing the family snow shovel. In a few days, they can afford to buy their own.

2. *Use supplies you have around the house.* Example: If you're starting a craft business, a family member might be glad to donate a box of fabric scraps that's been in the hall closet for the last 5 years.

3. *Buy only what you need to get started.* Example: The first bottle of window cleaner for your first window-washing job is a start-up cost. After that, window cleaner won't be a problem because you can buy it with the money you earn.

ESTIMATE OF STARTUP COSTS

1. Start-up costs for equipment:

   _____   _____

   _____   _____

   _____

   Subtotal: _____

2. Start-up costs for supplies:

   _____   _____

   _____   _____

   _____   _____

   _____   _____

   _____

   _____

   Subtotal: _____

3. Start-up costs for operations:

   _____   _____

   _____   _____

   _____   _____

   _____

   Subtotal: _____

4. Start-up costs for advertising:

   _____   _____

   _____   _____

   _____

   Subtotal: _____

   Grand total: _____

4. *Know the difference between needs and wants.* Example: It would be fun to have your own computer, but unless your business is computer services, you can probably get by with a calculator and notebook. Arrange to borrow time on your parent's computer when necessary.

Sometimes having a limited amount of money to start a business can be an asset. It forces you to think carefully about what you really need and requires that you spend every dime wisely. Some entrepreneurs call this being "lean and mean." I call it "thinking smart."

Starting your business the low-cost way cuts down on risk. Think about it. If your start-up list adds up to $200, but you only have $50 to invest, you have to make some "lean, mean decisions." You may have to do without some things you really wanted, but you have cut your investment and your risk by 75%. That's smart business.

Use the worksheet on page 88 to estimate your start-up costs. Include a copy of this estimate in your business plan.

2. Where can you get start-up money?

Most of the businesses recommended in *Fast Cash for Kids* can be started with very little money. For some young entrepreneurs, starting a business is as simple as using your allowance to print flyers advertising your Saturday morning puppet shows or pet-sitting service.

Businesses that involve selling a product cost more to start. If you dream of owning a T-shirt business or plan to sell baseball cards, your start-up costs will include some hefty expenses for the purchase of inventory.

If you find yourself short on capital to start your business, these suggestions may help you out:

1. Have a garage sale.
2. Do odd jobs to earn start-up money for your business.
3. Save money from your allowance or birthday gifts.
4. Find a partner with money to invest.
5. Negotiate a small loan from your parents.
6. Use your business plan to apply for a grant or loan.

Estimate of Operating Costs

1. **Fixed Operating Costs**

   Item: Cost:

   _____   _____

   _____   _____

   _____   _____

   _____   _____

   _____   _____

   _____   _____

   _____   _____

                                        Subtotal: _____

2. **Variable Operating Costs**

   Item: Cost:

   _____   _____

   _____   _____

   _____   _____

   _____   _____

   _____   _____

   _____   _____

   _____   _____

   _____   _____

   _____   _____

   _____   _____

   _____   _____

                                        Subtotal: _____

                                        Grand total: _____

Start-up money for young entrepreneurs often comes from a combination of sources. Your business plan should include a list of all your sources for start-up money and how much capital you estimate you can raise from each.

3. What are your monthly operating expenses?

After your initial start-up costs are taken care of, the income from your business should cover your monthly operating expenses. You can expect two types of ongoing expenses in your business: (1) fixed costs and (2) variable costs.

Fixed costs: Fixed costs are expenses that stay the same each month. Examples are rent, your basic monthly telephone bill, paging or answering service, and payments on the new computer you bought.

Variable costs: Variable costs go up or down, depending on the activity level of your business. Examples are office supplies, long-distance phone calls, the electric bill, and advertising.

Overhead is another word for operating costs. Sometimes business people say their business has too much overhead. That means they have too many operating expenses. Their expenses seem to hang "over their head," and they can't make enough profit.

To make good decisions about your business, you must have an accurate picture of your expenses. Use the worksheet on page 90 to develop a complete list of the monthly expenses for operating your business. Include a copy of this worksheet in your business plan.

4. What is your cost of goods?

The direct expenses you pay to produce, manufacture, or purchase the products you sell is called *cost of goods*.

Cost of goods for making a T-shirt might include the price of the shirt, paints, paint brushes, ribbon, and sequins. Cost of goods for baking a birthday cake would include the cost of the cake mix, eggs, oil, icing, decorations, and candles.

Cost of goods includes any raw materials, supplies, or equipment directly used to produce the product. It also includes wholesale prices and shipping charges to buy merchandise you plan to resale.

These are some ways young entrepreneurs use cost of goods to make business decisions:

> To know when to raise or lower prices
>
> To evaluate new products for profitability
>
> To know how much discount to allow a bargain hunter
>
> To figure how much income tax you owe

For every item you sell, you need a written record of the exact, to-the-penny cost of goods. A good way to keep these records is to set up a card file. On a card for each product or service, list the following information: name of product, description, date purchased or manufactured, number of units, wholesale price, cost of raw materials, shipping costs, any miscellaneous costs, and total cost of goods.

These records of your cost of goods should be updated as changes occur in the cost of goods. For example, during the winter holiday season, you can almost always buy semisweet chocolate chips for half price. It's a great time to bake and sell chocolate-chip cookies. However, if you continue the business year round, you will want to watch the price of chocolate chips closely. As soon as the prices go up, you'll need to update your records and adjust your prices to reflect the new cost of goods.

5. What is your selling price?

One of the trickiest problems of business for young entrepreneurs is setting prices. Making a profit in your business depends on setting your prices high enough to cover your expenses and time, yet low enough that the customer feels he's getting a bargain. That's hard to do.

Steve Mariotti, president and founder of the National Foundation for Teaching Entrepreneurship (NFTE), says, "Making a profit in business always starts with correct pricing." He teaches young entrepreneurs who enroll in his classes a pricing concept he calls "The Economics of One Unit." These are the four steps to follow:

Step 1: Define one unit of your product. That's easy if you're selling ties or watches. One unit is one tie or one watch. But if you're selling cookies, one unit is harder to define. Is one unit one cookie? Four cookies? A dozen cookies? Each variation of your product requires a separate analysis of its unit price.

Step 2: Calculate the exact cost of goods for one unit. If you buy candy by the bag, determine the cost of one piece of candy. If you're selling muffins, figure out what it costs to make a batch of muffins. Then figure how much one muffin costs.

Step 3: Set the selling price. Steve Mariotti teaches young entrepreneurs to double the cost of goods to get the selling price. So if the cost of goods for one watch is $5, the selling price is $10. The gross profit (profit before operating expenses) on each watch is $5.

Step 4: Determine your net profit. Operating expenses such as telephone, advertising, and office supplies indirectly contribute to the cost of producing your product. Estimate your average monthly operating expenses and divide by the number of watches you sell per month. This gives you the per-unit operating cost for each watch. Calculate your net profit by subtracting the per-unit operating cost from the gross profit on each watch.

For example, if the per-unit operating cost for each watch is $1, subtract $1 from your $5 gross profit. Your net profit is $4 or 40%, a respectable per-unit profit that anyone would be pleased to make. Now you know that $10 is an acceptable selling price for your watches.

Setting prices on services: Service businesses like snow shoveling or cleaning aquariums have almost no overhead costs. Instead of the cost analysis method of setting prices, a service business primarily bases its prices on a fair wage per hour.

First estimate the time you expect the job to take (2 hours to shovel the driveway). Then multiply by the amount you wish to make per hour ($4.50 an hour × 2 hours. = $9). Add the cost of equipment or supplies ($1 for wear and tear on the snow shovel). Your total price for the job is $10.

Check your competition: After you have figured the selling price of your product or service, you need to check your price against the going rate. How does your price compare to what others are charging for similar products or services? If your price is lower than everyone else's, you may be undervaluing your product. If your price is higher than everyone else, you may be spending too much on supplies or charging too much for labor. Look for ways to cut costs.

The first few times you talk to customers about money, you may feel a little unsure about quoting your fees. Remind yourself that your fees are based on careful research. You can assure your customers that your rates are fair when compared to what others charge.

A price list: Another way to boost your confidence is to make a written list of the services you provide and your rates. When you start discussing money with your customers, hand them a copy of your price list. Your customers will appreciate the professional way you handle your business, and you will be happier with what you earn.

PRICE LIST: CALL-A-KID YARD SERVICE

Service	Price
Mowing, small yard	$10.00
Mowing, large yard	$20.00
Edging	$5.00
Weeding flower beds	$0.50 per square feet
Raking leaves	$1.00 per bag
Snow removal, small area	$2.00
Snow removal, large areas	$4.50 per hour

Remember that once you make a deal with a customer for a certain price, you must honor what you said even if the job takes longer or the supplies cost more than you expected. So do your research. Then create a price list and include it in your business plan.

6. How much do you have to sell to break even?

Suppose you sold 50 leather belts, 50 hand-strung necklaces, and 50 pounds of gourmet chocolates from your flea market booth last month. It sounds like you made a lot of money. But before you can take any money out of the business, you must pay your cost of goods and operating expenses. The amount you have left after that is your profit.

This is the formula for figuring profit:

Income - Expenses = Profit

Income = Everything you get paid

Expenses = Everything you spend to run your business

Profit = The money you have left after you subtract your
expenses from your income

Most businesses don't make a profit when they first start out. During the start-up phase, the first big goal is to reach the *break-even point,* the happy day when your income covers all the expenses and you are no longer operating at a loss.

It is very important to know how many sales you have to make to reach the break-even point every month. Steve Mariotti of NFTE advises young entrepreneurs to use a system he calls the Break-Even Analysis. These are the steps he recommends:

1. Estimate your monthly operating expenses. (Don't confuse cost of goods with operating expenses.)

2. Divide your operating expenses by the gross profit you make every time you sell one unit.

3. The result is the number of units you must sell to cover all expenses and reach the break-even point.

Continuing the earlier example of the watch-selling business, let say you have $50 monthly operating expenses. The gross profit on each watch is $5, which you can use to pay the operating expenses. If you divide $50 by $5, you will find you need to sell 10 watches to reach the break-even point each month.

This section of your business plan should include an analysis of your break-even point and how you plan to achieve sales to cover your expenses.

7. What are your sales goals?

When a business first starts, reaching the break-even point is a big day. But no one wants to continue operating a business at the break-even point (the zero profit level). What is your goal for profit levels in your business? How many more units do you have to sell each month to reach that goal?

Fair profit: For some people, profit is a negative word that means you took advantage of other people to benefit yourself. This is not the kind of profit we are speaking of in this book. We are looking for a fair profit earned by providing a product or service that benefits the consumer.

All young entrepreneurs deserve to make a fair wage or a fair profit from their work. If you don't make a profit, you won't be able to stay in business very long. Then the community will lose out on the contribution your business would have provided.

SALES GOALS WORKSHEET

1. Define one unit of your product: _____

2. Determine the cost of goods for one unit: _____

3. To set the selling price, multiply cost of goods by 2.

   Cost of goods per unit × 2 = _____

   (selling price)

4. Determine gross profit on each unit by subtracting cost of goods from selling price.

   Selling price of one unit: _____

   Less cost of goods per unit: _____

   Gross profit per unit: _____

5. Determine your total monthly operating expenses.

   Fixed costs: _____

   Variable costs: _____

   Total operating expenses: _____

6. How many units do you have to sell this month to break even? Divide operating expense by gross profit per unit.

   Monthly operating expense: _____

   Divided by gross profit per unit: _____

   Number of units to break even: _____

7. Monthly profit desired (after expenses): _____

   Divided by gross profit per unit: _____

   Number of additional units I must sell this month to reach my monthly profit goals: _____

The worksheet on the previous page (page 96) will help you determine your break-even point, then go beyond that point to a level of profit you will enjoy. Successful entrepreneurs always use goals as targets for progress. State your goals for sales and profits in measurable terms, and include them in this section of your business plan.

8. How will you set up a bookkeeping system?

As your business grows, it will be totally impossible to keep all the information about your business in your head.

Smart entrepreneurs set up a bookkeeping system to record and manage all the money that comes in or goes out of their business.

In bookkeeping terms, "books" are whatever you write your records on. Your books may be kept on sheets of paper, in a notebook, in a card file, on a ledger, or on a computer disk. Your system doesn't have to be elaborate or formal, just as long as every business transaction is recorded. This is the only way to know exactly how much profit your business is earning.

It may surprise you to know that many adult entrepreneurs use the "shoe box" system of record keeping. Here's what you need to set up a shoe box system:

_____ *Two shoe boxes:* If you don't have shoe boxes, use small school supply boxes or large envelopes.

_____ *Customer receipt forms:* You can buy a receipt book at the office supply store, print receipts from your computer, or photocopy our sample on the next page (page 98).

_____ *Payout records:* These are just 3 × 5 cards or small slips of paper with the words "Payout Record" written at the top.

_____ *A bookkeeping ledger or spiral notebook:* You can buy a standard bookkeeping ledger at the office supply store or use a spiral notebook. This book is very important because it is your bookkeeping journal.

_____ *Large envelopes:* Save money by reusing large envelopes you get in the mail. This system doesn't have to look good to work.

CUSTOMER RECEIPT

Business name: _____

Address: _____

Phone: _____

Date: _____ Receipt number: _____

Customer's name: _____

Customer address: _____

_____

For: Amount received:

_____   _____

_____   _____

_____   _____

_____   _____

_____   _____

_____   _____

_____   _____

                        Subtotal: _____

                        Sales tax: _____

                        Total paid: _____

Sales representative: _____

_____

Notes: _____

_____

_____

_____

_____

HOW TO RUN A SHOE BOX RECORD-KEEPING SYSTEM

1. Label one shoe box "Income" and the other "Expenses."

2. Each time you get paid for a sale or a job, make two copies of your customer's receipt. One copy goes to the customer and the other goes in your box marked "Income."

3. Each time you spend money on your business, save your store receipt. Then write up a "payout record" noting the date, how much you spent, and what you bought. Attach the store receipt to the payout record and put it in the box marked "Expenses."

4. Open the ledger and label the very front page "Income Journal." Turn to the first two facing pages of the Income Journal and label your columns as suggested here.

Date	Source	Taxable sale	Sales tax	Nontaxable sale	Total

Each week, you will take all your receipts out of the box marked "Income" and list each transaction in the Income Journal. Income you receive for service jobs is listed as a nontaxable sale.

5. Now open the ledger to the very back page and label it "Expense Journal." Working from the back of the ledger toward the middle, turn to the first two facing pages of your Expense Journal. Label columns for your most frequent expenses or as suggested here.

Date	Paid to	Cost of goods	Operating expense	Other expense

PROFIT & LOSS STATEMENT

For month of: _____

Income:

Source: Amount:

_____   _____

_____   _____

_____   _____

                              Total Income: _____

Cost of Goods:

                                                 Amount:

Work supplies: _____

Equipment: _____

Materials: _____

Other : _____   _____

Operating Expenses:

Office supplies: _____

Printing: _____

Postage: _____

Phone: _____

Other : _____   _____

                          Total Expenses: _____

(Subtract Total Expenses from Total Income.)

Profit (or loss) for this month: _____

Each week, you will take all your payout records out of the box marked "Expenses" and list each transaction in the Expense Journal.

6. At the end of each month, total the Income Journal and the Expense Journal. Make new pages for the next month. Store each month's receipts and payout records in a envelope marked with the date and contents.

7. At the end of each month, you should also prepare a special report called a "Profit & Loss Statement" (sometimes called a P&L). The P&L statement is a short, one-page summary of your business transactions for the month. The formula for creating a Profit & Loss statement is the same you've already been using: Income - Expenses = Profit. Use the form on the previous page to figure your monthly Profit & Loss statement. As the months go by, it will be very helpful to compare your monthly P&Ls and see how your business is growing and changing.

Using a computer to do your bookkeeping: If you have access to a computer, you may want to use one of the popular bookkeeping software programs such as *Quicken* or *Microsoft Money* to manage your business records. These programs are a little complicated to set up, but they are extremely helpful. Generating a monthly P&L statement, for example, takes only the click of a button. Most of the software programs also create wonderful bar graphs and pie charts to go with your financial reports. However, the biggest advantage of bookkeeping on computer is the ease of preparing data for income tax reports.

Keeping records for income tax: If your business is successful and you make a profit of $400 a year, you are required by federal law to file three tax forms:

Form 1040, the two-page U.S. Individual Tax Return

Schedule C, to report profit (or loss) from business

Schedule SE, to figure social security taxes due on self-employment income

Because you will be allowed to subtract the standard personal deduction on Form 1040, you probably won't owe as much tax as you might think. In 1994, the standard deduction was $3,800. That means you would have to make a profit of over $3,800 to owe any federal income tax. However, you may owe a small amount of self-employment tax.

Business owners who make a profit of more than $8,000 per year are required to pay part of their taxes every few months. Form 1040-ES, Estimated Tax for Individuals, contains the schedule and instructions for filing quarterly income tax reports.

Some states also have a state income tax. It is your responsibility as a business owner to know which tax laws apply to you. It is also very important that you keep good records of your income and expenses, so you can prove that the amounts you show on your tax reports are accurate.

Every year the government prints books that explain changes in the tax laws and tell how to fill out the tax forms. You can get free copies of these books at your post office or public library. If you have additional tax questions, you should consult a professional tax preparer, a CPA, or the Internal Revenue Service.

9. What business forms do you need?

Never rely on verbal agreements alone to conduct your business affairs. Every sale, order, or business transaction should have some kind of paperwork to back it up. This "paper trail" helps avoid disagreements and possible financial losses.

Depending on the type of business you own, forms to give bids, create contracts, tell customers what they owe, or to order from suppliers may be useful. Always make at least two copies of the completed form, one for your records and one (or more) for the customer.

Purchase orders: When you want to buy something from another business for your business, you list it on a purchase order. Many suppliers and wholesalers require a signed and numbered purchase order every time you place an order. You can buy packages of numbered purchase order forms at the office supply store.

When you make out the purchase order, you keep one copy for yourself and send two copies to the supplier. If you have to call the supplier later to discuss an error in the shipment, they will ask for your "P.O. number." P.O. is short for purchase order. The number on your purchase order helps them locate the exact order you wish to discuss.

Bid forms: A business that performs services of any kind may find bid forms useful. These forms, also called *estimate forms,* can be purchased at an office supply store or created on your computer. You use the form to write up a description of the job you are proposing to do, your expenses, and your fees. If you operate a pool-cleaning service, for example, a customer may request a written bid from you and several other companies. After comparing bids, the customer will chose one company to do the work. If you get the job, you may wish to have the customer sign a contract before you begin.

Contracts: Lunch Box on Wheels, the catering service in Chapter 5, has customers sign a contract when they book a dinner. Liza and LaRae spend a lot of time and money preparing a dinner for 200 people. It would be a disaster if they showed up with the food, and the customers said they had changed their minds. Most caterers also require customers to pay a deposit when the contract is signed.

A signed contract is your assurance that the customer really wants the work done and intends to pay you when you finish. Office supply stores have sample contract forms, but it is often easier to use your computer to produce contracts.

This is a checklist of points you may wish to include in your contract:

_____ Date contract was written

_____ Name and address of customer

_____ Date service is to begin and end

_____ Place service will be provided

_____ Equipment you provide

_____ Equipment the customer provides

_____ Supplies needed and who buys them

_____ Detailed description of services

_____ Detailed description of products

_____ Special instructions

_____ Terms of payment

_____ Amount of deposit

_____ Date payment is due

_____ Signature of customer agreeing to terms

If you are dealing with larger amounts of money and want to be sure your agreement covers every legal aspect, you should have a lawyer write your contract.

CUSTOMER INVOICE

Business name: _____

Address: _____

City: _____ State: _____ Zip: _____

Phone: _____

Invoice date:_____ Invoice number: _____

Customer: _____

_____

_____

Total due upon receipt: $ _____

Item: Amount due:

1. _____ $ _____

2. _____   _____

3. _____   _____

4. _____   _____

5. _____   _____

6. _____   _____

7. _____   _____

8. _____   _____

Subtotal: _____

Amount paid: _____

Balance due: _____

Thank You for Your Business!

Signed: _____

Invoices: When you finish a job or deliver a product, you get paid by presenting a bill. An invoice is a form for telling customers what they owe. When they receive the invoice, they know it's time to get out the checkbook and pay the bill.

A sample customer invoice form is provided on the preceding page (page 104). You can also buy invoices at the office supply store, or print them on your computer. It is a good idea to number your invoices. Then, if you need to discuss a bill with a customer, you can refer to the invoice number.

Most customers pay promptly, particularly if you deliver the invoice in person and stand there looking expectant. If you mail the invoice and the customer doesn't pay within 10 days, send a second copy as a reminder. Office supply stores have stamps or stickers to use on the bottom of invoices to prompt slow-paying customers. You are most likely to get paid if you remain courteous and friendly, no matter how many notices you have to send. However, you should carefully consider whether you want to work for this customer again in the future.

Monthly statements: In addition to the invoices you provide after each sale, your regular customers will appreciate receiving a monthly statement. A monthly statement is a summary of all activity on their account for the month and the current balance due. Some customers like to pay their bill when they receive their monthly statement.

Office supply stores have standard forms for monthly statements. However, the easiest way to create customer statements is on your computer. Some bookkeeping programs even generate monthly statements for your customers automatically. Above all, sending monthly statements is a courtesy to your customers and the mark of a professionally operated business.

10. What bank do you plan to use?

If you don't already have a savings account when you start your business, you should open one immediately. A savings account gives you a safe place to keep the money you earn. It also establishes you as an account holder at the bank. Then when a customer gives you a check, you will have a place to cash it.

Not every young entrepreneur needs a checking account. To open an account in your business name, you will be required to show the bank a copy of your DBA form. One disadvantage of a business checking account is that the service charges are higher

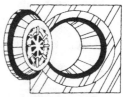

than for personal accounts. However, a checking account is an excellent record-keeping tool for your business if you faithfully deposit all income and pay all expenses through the account.

Fees, service charges, and interest vary widely from bank to bank. Before you choose a bank to handle your business account, do some shopping around.

Checklist for Comparing Banks:

_____ What is the minimum deposit to open an account?

_____ What rate of interest is paid on savings accounts?

_____ What are the service charges on checking accounts?

_____ Are there extra fees on commercial checking accounts?

_____ Is a parent required to cosign on checking accounts?

_____ Are the location and hours convenient?

_____ Is the bank friendly to young people?

Many banks throughout the U.S. are starting to think more about serving the needs of young people. Some have special tellers for youth, computers with games that teach math and money, and workshops to help kids understand banking.

The Young Americans Bank in Denver, Colorado, which opened in 1987, was the first commercial bank for young people under the age of 22. Anyone more than 12 years old can open a checking account. They also give business loans to young people and offer a charge card with a $200 limit. You don't have to live in Denver to start an account. They have customers from as far away as West Germany. For information on banking by mail, write Young Americans Bank, 311 Steele Street, Denver, CO 80206.

Your business plan should include a listing of your bank accounts, the purpose of each account, and the name and address of your bank.

11. How will you maintain a positive cash flow?

When your business starts making money, it will be very tempting to spend every penny on things you've been wanting. If you do, you will endanger the future of your business.

Suppose you invest $50 you saved from birthdays and allowances to start a T-shirt business. You buy supplies to make eight shirts. Everyone loves the shirts, and you sell them all in a week and have $120 in your pocket. That is the exact amount you need to buy the new pair of boots you've been wanting. So you spend all the money on the boots. Now you have a pair of boots valued at $120, but no money to buy more supplies and run your business. Your business has already gone broke.

You can change this story to have a happier ending. You invested $50 and made $120, so your profit was $70. Since you are a smart business person, you put the $70 profit in the bank. Then use the $50 to buy more supplies and make another $120, giving you another $70 profit. Now you're on a roll. You've still got your $50 start-up money, and you have $140 profit in the bank. You can buy the boots for $120 and have $20 left for emergencies or to buy more T-shirt supplies. Your business is steadily growing.

The first rule of having a healthy cash flow in your business is: Never spend your operating capital. Always keep a reserve of cash to buy more supplies and operate your business. This is known as maintaining "a positive cash flow."

Maintaining a positive cash flow requires thoughtful planning. The best tool for planning your spending and saving is a *budget*. A budget is simply a written plan that balances the INcome and OUTgo (cash flow) of money in your business. On the next page (page 108) is a worksheet for planning your monthly budget.

Some young people don't like the word *budget* because it sounds like a diet, which means "I can't do things I want to do." Remember, this is not a budget someone else makes you follow. You are the creator of this budget, so you determine how much you want to restrict or release your cash flow.

If you have trouble balancing your budget (we all do), there are three things you can do:

1. Earn more.
2. Spend less.
3. Set priorities.

Setting priorities is a valuable skill in business. Make a list of all the things you want or need. Then number the items in order of their importance. Then you will know which expenditures you can do without or delay until you earn more money.

BUDGET WORKSHEET

For month of: _____

Possible Income:

Amounts:

Business income: $ _____

_____

_____

_____

(Estimate the number of sales and multiply by average income per sale.)

Other income:

Allowance: _____

Gifts: _____

Other: _____

Total estimated income: _____

Possible Expenses:

Amounts:

Business expenses: $ _____

Cost of goods: _____

Operating expenses: _____

Other: _____

Personal expenses: $ _____

Savings: _____

Giving to help others: _____
(usually 10% of your income)

Other: _____

Total estimated expenses: _____

Total income: _____ **Total expenses:** _____

Your budget is a very important part of your business plan. When you are satisfied with the final version of your budget, include a copy in your business plan.

12. How much money do you need to borrow?

It is always best to finance your business without borrowing money. Earlier in this chapter, a number of ways to raise start-up capital were suggested. However, if you are planning to apply for a loan, questions 12 through 16 will help you convince lenders you are a good risk.

The first step in a loan request is to state the amount you wish to borrow. This figure should be backed up with facts about your start-up costs, operating expenses, and cost of goods. You should also show how much capital you are personally investing.

13. How do you plan to use the money you borrow?

Using the profit & loss statement in this chapter as a pattern, create a detailed plan showing how you will spend the money from the loan to start the business. List supplies, equipment, advertising costs, printing, and any other items necessary for the start-up. Lenders want to know that you have researched your business thoroughly, and they want to be convinced you will be responsible with their money.

14. How will you repay the loan?

Getting a loan is a serious financial obligation. You must have a step-by-step plan for repaying the money in a timely manner. Lenders want to know these things:

1. How much you will pay weekly or monthly
2. The rate of interest you are proposing
3. How long it will take to repay the money
4. Due dates for payments
5. Penalties for late payments

Most lenders also want to see a report of your estimated cash flow for the next year. The best way to create this report is to make 12 copies of the profit & loss statement. Then create an estimate of your cash flow for every month of the coming year. Be sure to list your loan payments as part of your monthly operating expenses, and show that you expect adequate income to cover the payments.

Many business owners like to prepare cash flow projections for the coming year even if they are not applying for a loan. These reports are very useful for studying the potential profit on a new business idea, service, or product.

15. What can you offer as collateral?

Collateral is something you own that is of equal value to the amount of the loan. You must promise in writing to give this item of collateral to the lender if you default on the loan. Things you might use for collateral are a bicycle, watch, stereo, computer, CD player, or baseball card collection.

Your loan proposal should describe the item you are offering as collateral and provide proof of its value. Many lenders hold the item of collateral in their possession until the loan is repaid. Never offer equipment you need for running your business as collateral on a loan.

16. What is your evidence of financial responsibility?

The business plan you have written is tremendous evidence you have the ability to start a business and run it responsibly. In addition to all the research and reports in your business plan, a lender will want to know about your financial history. In other words, who have you borrowed money from in the past? Did you pay the loans back on time?

The people who have loaned you money before are your *credit references.* When reviewing your loan application, lenders often contact these references and ask about your payment record.

Your loan request should include a list of at least five credit references, their addresses and phone numbers, the amount of the loans, and when they were paid off. Many young entrepreneurs list loans from parents, grandparents, relatives, and friends of the family. If you have been in business for awhile and have bought goods from a supplier, you may also list that supplier as a credit reference. Your bank is a good credit reference if you have had a checking account for 6 months or more.

WHAT HAPPENS AFTER THE LOAN IS APPROVED?

The lender may or may not accept the exact terms you propose in your loan request. When the loan is approved, ask to see a copy of the contract so that you can review the terms before signing. If you have any problem understanding the contract, ask someone you trust to review the loan papers with you.

Keep in mind that until you are 18, you are considered a minor, and no contract you sign is legally binding. For this reason, some lenders may require that your parents cosign with you on the loan.

Most loans for young entrepreneurs are informal loans from parents or relatives. Always insist that terms for any loan be stated in writing, even if the loan is only $25 and it's coming from your parents. Written terms protect both the lender and the borrower from future confusion and misunderstandings about money.

CELEBRATE YOUR SUCCESS!

You deserve to pat yourself on the back today. It took a lot of energy and determination to follow all the steps in Chapters 5, 6, and 7. Because of your hard work, you have completed your business plan. You have created an outline of the organization and operation of your business, the marketing of your product, and how you will handle your finances. You are on your way to success.

The next chapter explains details about the everyday management of your business. Congratulations! You are now ready to be your own boss.

·8·

HOW TO BE YOUR OWN BOSS

JASON MILLER BEGAN HIS CAREER AS AN ENTREPRENEUR BY SELLING ICE CREAM IN front of his home in Livingston, New Jersey, during the summer he was 6 years old. The sun melted the ice cream so fast that he had to keep running in the house to put the nearly melted bars in the freezer and get new bars to refill the ice bucket in his stand. Jason could see that a summer ice cream stand wasn't a long-term business.

When he was 8 years old, Jason decided he wanted to start a real business. This time he chose a product people need year round: computer services. Using the initials from his name, Jason named his business J M Industries and made some flyers advertising private computer tutoring. Then he walked all over his community, placing flyers on bulletin boards and counters and talking to anyone who would listen to his pitch.

Soon adults were calling to inquire about tutoring. Jason answered the private phone line in his bedroom, "J M Industries." He practiced lowering his voice and did his best to convince potential customers he was businesslike and professional. But it was hard to overcome being 8 years old, even if he was an expert on all the most popular software programs and had written programs to handle the office work in his dad's medical practice.

Jason didn't give up. More than anything else, Jason wanted the freedom of owning his own business and being his own boss. He wanted to make decisions and take total responsibility for the results. And he wanted to use his knowledge of computer technology to help other people.

Business was slow compared to what Jason had envisioned, but he still earned enough to have all the spending money he needed. As Jason's reputation for solving computer problems grew, customers started calling for other kinds of help. Soon Jason was assisting clients in the setup of new computer systems, repairing computers, and trouble-shooting software problems. By the time he was 11, Jason had a license to sell used computer equipment, and J M Industries was growing rapidly.

Today Jason is 14 and J M Industries has celebrated its sixth anniversary. Jason mostly sells new computer systems and provides installation, upgrading, repair, and tutoring services. His bookkeeping is done on computer (naturally) and keeps track of each client's annual purchases. Each time a customer spends $1,000, the computer prints a $10 gift certificate to be mailed as a Thank You from Jason. The computer also tells Jason how much sales tax and income tax to set aside from each sale. Jason never tells anyone exactly how much he earns, but he is one of the few young entrepreneurs who pays quarterly income tax, sales tax, and tariffs on imports.

Jason's advice for other young entrepreneurs is, "Don't be afraid to learn by trial and error. If they don't teach what you want to learn in school, go out and learn it yourself."

THE OFFICIAL OPENING OF YOUR BUSINESS

After you have followed all the steps in Chapters 5, 6, and 7 to organize your business and write a business plan, it's time to announce that you are officially open. Some business owners do this by have a grand-opening event. Some, like Jason Miller, just start passing out advertisements and telling people about their services.

A grand opening can be a party, an open house, an official ceremony, or just going out for pizza with your friends. The purpose is to launch your business and tell potential customers you are open.

These are some suggestions for ways to officially open your business:

1. Invite all your friends and relatives to a grand-opening celebration. Give demonstrations of your product or service and serve refreshments. Hand out lots of flyers and ask everyone to tell others about your business.

GRAND OPENING SALE!

2. Get your friends to help you stage an official ribbon-cutting ceremony. Make a giant pair of scissors out of cardboard. Have two people stretch a wide ribbon across your front door or business location. Take pictures of friends helping you "cut" the ribbon to officially "open the doors." Be sure to send your story to the local papers.

3 Host a come-and-go open house to celebrate your new business. Display your products and give away free samples, business cards, and brochures.

4. Send out a special letter to all your friends, relatives, and neighbors announcing the opening of your business. Include coupons for introductory specials.

5. Have calendars, pens, refrigerator magnets, or other small gifts printed with your business name and information. Go door-to-door in your neighborhood handing out these gifts and announcing the opening of your business. Be sure to take order forms along, just in case you get a new customer right on the spot.

AN OFFICIAL TITLE FOR THE OWNER

Once your business is open, you are going to have some management decisions to make. After all, you're the boss, and the total operation of the business is now up to you.

Big corporations have a special title for the person who manages the business and makes the decisions. That person is called the chief executive officer, or CEO. You can call yourself the CEO, the president, the owner, the proprietor, or the manager. Whatever you choose, it's a nice touch of professionalism to use your title on your business cards and all your official correspondence.

What's most important is that you realize all the management is up to you. You're the leader. Whatever happens, whatever growth occurs, whatever profit is made is totally in your hands.

This is the time to think carefully about the future. If you're going to lead, you've got to know where you're going. That means setting goals.

ANOTHER DIMENSION

Ron Brown of Derby, Kansas, decided he wanted to become a mobile disk jockey (DJ) when he was in seventh grade. There were two major obstacles blocking his goal: (1) He didn't know how to be a DJ and (2) he didn't have $1,500 to buy the necessary equipment.

Assessing the situation, Ron figured it would take him awhile, but he could overcome these problems. First he set a goal to earn enough money to buy the equipment. Then he got a paper route and started saving. He constantly looked for ways to earn extra money. At one point, he had three paper routes and an office job, plus he attended school full time.

While he was working toward the start-up money, Ron set another goal, to learn all he could about being a disk jockey. Every chance he got to meet a DJ or watch a DJ in action, Ron was there taking note of details and asking questions. Occasionally, one disk jockey he made friends with would spend extra time explaining techniques and tips of the trade. Meanwhile, Ron continued to amass a large collection of music that would appeal to any audience.

By ninth grade, Ron was ready to launch his business. He named it Another Dimension Mobile D.J. Service. After he began to establish a reputation and had an income of about $300 a month coming in from doing school parties, Ron set some new goals. He decided that while he was still living at home, he would reinvest all the money he earned back into the business to buy more equipment and eventually hire other disk jockeys to work for him.

Today Ron is a senior in high school, owns two complete sound systems, and manages bookings for himself and one other disk jockey he has trained. Each year he is in business he sets one big major goal to accomplish. His next goal is a third sound system and a third DJ on the road.

HOW TO GET WHAT YOU WANT

Jason Miller and Ron Brown succeeded in business because they were sure about what they wanted to achieve. Jason wanted to be his own boss more than anything else in the world. He set smaller goals to help reach his big goal. Some of his goals were to:

1. Get a license to sell computer equipment.

2. Sell clients more than $1,000 in merchandise.

3. Keep accurate records and pay his taxes.

Ron wanted to be a mobile disk jockey. He set goals at every stage of his business. Some of the goals he achieved were:

1. Earn enough money to buy start-up equipment.

2. Meet other disk jockeys and learn what they do.

3. Buy a second sound system.

4. Have another disk jockey working for him.

Like Jason Miller and Ron Brown, you will get what you want when you have a burning desire to achieve your goal. Successful entrepreneurs are always motivated by a strong desire to achieve. They say to themselves, "No matter how long it takes or how hard I have to work, I will do this."

The determination to succeed always results in action. In other words, if you really want something, you'll start taking action to get it. Your brain will start searching for ways to reach the goal. The steps to achievement will become very clear, and you will be anxious to get busy.

Actions that are fueled by a strong desire to achieve almost always "start a fire." In other words, they get results that lead to other results. Here's an example. You set a goal to sell one customer $1,000 in merchandise. You accomplish that goal, and you are thrilled with success. It is so exciting to know you can sell $1,000 in merchandise to one customer that you want to go out and sell $2,000 in merchandise to the next customer. Your fire is lit. In fact, it's raging!

HOW TO BE THE ONE WHO ACHIEVES

Success always leads to more success. If you want to achieve outstanding success in your personal life, school, or business enterprise, practice these steps:

1. Recognize what it is you really have a burning desire to achieve.

2. Write your goal on a 3 × 5 card and carry it with you everywhere you go. Read it several times a day and begin looking for ways to reach the goal.

GOAL WORKSHEET

Goal setting is the number one tool for good business management. Use this worksheet to set goals for sales, income, cost control, marketing, or the future growth of your business.

List three goals you would like to achieve during the next 3 months.

Goal #1: _____

Goal #2: _____

Goal #3: _____

List three things you need to do to achieve goal #1.

     Step: Date to complete:

1. _____   _____

2. _____   _____

3. _____   _____

List three things you need to do to achieve goal #2.

     Step: Date to complete:

1. _____   _____

2. _____   _____

3. _____   _____

List three things you need to do to achieve goal #3.

     Step: Date to complete:

1. _____   _____

2. _____   _____

3. _____   _____

Copy this worksheet and use it again to set personal goals for school, career, self improvement, etc.

3. As ideas to achieve the goal become clear to you, write the steps on the card.

4. Make a promise to yourself to do one thing every day toward reaching your goal. (You can do more if you wish.)

5. Each time you take a step toward completing the goal, put a checkmark by that step on the card.

6. When you accomplish the goal, write the date you reached it in red letters at the top and tack the card on the mirror in your room. Look at it every day and say, "I am a person who sets and achieves exciting goals."

7. Then write a new goal on another 3 × 5 card and start again. Expect to achieve your desires.

Each time you use this system to set and accomplish a goal, your fire is going to burn stronger and stronger. You are going to be like a rocket on a launching pad, blasting off into the Earth's atmosphere, overcoming gravity and breaking through the frontiers of space. Nothing will hold you back.

If they don't teach what you need to know about computers in school, you'll be like Jason Miller and learn it yourself. If you need more training to be a disk jockey or a fashion designer, you'll find someone who is already a success in the field and start asking questions. If one customer says No, you'll keep on knocking on doors until the next one says Yes. Enthusiasm gives you the desire to work longer, harder, and more diligently than any of your competitors. And you will be the one who ultimately succeeds.

MAKING EXECUTIVE DECISIONS

Goal setting is the number one tool of business management.

Use the goal worksheet on the preceding page (page 118) to concentrate on 3 major goals you wish to achieve in the next 3 months. This worksheet can be copied and used over and over to set goals for your business as well as your school, family, and personal life.

These are the top seven goals most young entrepreneurs list for business and personal achievement:

1. To have a steady income

2. To use time wisely

3. To control spending

4. To reach a short-term savings goal

5. To save toward a long-term goal

6. To reinvest money back into the business

7. To prepare for a career

GOAL #1: TO HAVE A STEADY INCOME

When most young entrepreneurs picture success for their business, they picture lots of customers, lots of sales, and lots of money.

When setting your income goals, keep in mind that growing a business is much like growing a garden. First you plant the seeds, then little plants come up, then you have to water and take care of them, and finally one day you are able to pick the vegetables and enjoy your labors.

Businesses also go through stages of growth. There will be times when you won't be able to take money from the business for personal expenses. As you read the following descriptions of the phases of business, ask yourself two questions: (1) How much profit can I expect at this stage? (2) What is the wisest way to use the money?

PHASES OF BUSINESS GROWTH

Research phase: Expenses may include taking a class, buying books, postage, phone, and photocopying. There is no product to sell and no income. You operate on savings.

Start-up phase: Having faith that sales will result, you spend money to begin the business. If the start-up money is borrowed, you will have to pay it back before you can take any income for yourself. The business is not yet making a profit.

Break-even point: This is a happy day. This is the day income from the business starts covering all expenses. You may not be making much profit, but you are no longer operating at a loss.

Early growth: Sales are increasing gradually and some profits are seen. However, the money almost always goes back into the business to buy more equipment or supplies.

Steady growth: You've discovered marketing strategies that work, and new customers are being added weekly. The business is supporting itself, and you are now able to take some money out for personal use.

Maturity: You've developed a list of regular customers and are continuing to add new customers through referrals and marketing efforts. Business operations are mostly smooth, and you have money to both to reinvest and spend for personal use.

Decline: Market changes or changes in your personal life decrease profits from the business. You either decide to take the business in a new direction and go back into a stage of growth, or you let the business phase itself out.

Growing a business requires constantly asking yourself, What's next? How can I improve? Where do I expand? Successful entrepreneurs don't sit and wait for something to happen. They set goals and go after the things they want.

GOAL #2: TO USE TIME WISELY

Although written goals set the course for the future of your business, achieving those goals depends on wise use of time and resources.

Successful young entrepreneurs must learn to balance the demands of their business with the demands of school, family, and personal life. To keep your business running smoothly, you have to perform the work you've promised your customers. But you also need time to do your homework, go to band practice, participate in sports, and be with your friends. Sometimes you just need time to do nothing.

Fifth-grader Melissa Gollick, owner of MelMaps, a computer graphics company that makes vicinity and location maps for real estate brokers and businesses in Denver, Colorado, has worked out a way to solve her time conflicts. When she started her business 2 years ago, Melissa had a talk with her parents and set priorities about how she would use her after-school hours. First is homework. Second is family activities, unless she has a client that needs a map the next day. In that case, making the map takes priority and family is third. Melissa also sings in the

Colorado Children's Chorale and enjoys hiking, biking, swimming, and going to summer camp. All these personal interests are worked in after the jobs she has promised her clients are completed.

Conflicts of priorities waste time. Talk with someone you trust about what comes first in your life. Is it school? Choir? Cheerleading? Personal fitness? Where does your business fit into your list of priorities? Make a list of all the activities that are important to you. Then number each activity in order of its priority. Make your choices now, and you won't waste time and energy later trying to solve conflicts.

These are the three time management tools most often used by young entrepreneurs:

1. *Master "to do" list:* Study the goals you have written for your business, and create a master list of things to do in the next 30 days, 60 days, and 90 days. Keep this list in a folder with your goals worksheets. This is your master plan for achievement.

2. *An appointment calendar:* Buy an inexpensive appointment calendar that is small enough to carry with you everywhere. First write in all your important school deadlines, practice schedules, social commitments, and dates you don't want to forget. Then write in realistic dates to accomplish the important items on your master "to do" list. Use the calendar faithfully to keep track of appointments with customers and deadlines to have jobs completed or orders delivered.

3. *Daily checklist:* At the end of every day, look back over your master "to do" list, and write down the five most important things you need to do tomorrow. Number these items in order of importance. At the beginning of the next day, start on the first thing on the list. Don't worry if you don't accomplish all five things every day. You will always be working on the one that's top priority.

GOAL #3: TO CONTROL SPENDING

When you work hard to earn your own money, you want to be sure it is managed well. But even when you set goals and make good plans to save and budget, it sometimes seems as if money has wings. Where does it all go?

If you never seem to know where your money goes, try keeping a money diary for a few weeks. Here's how to get started:

1. Use a small notebook you can carry with you everywhere. On the first page, write the date and the words "Beginning Balance." To the right, enter the total amount of money in your possession today.

2. Every time you spend money, write the date, the amount, and a description of the expense in your diary. Subtract each expenditure from your balance.

3. Every time you receive money or earn money, write the date, the amount, and the source in your diary. Keep a running total of your balance at all times.

4. At the end of the first week, study the entries in your notebook. Group your expenses into categories such as business expenses, hobby supplies, clothes, entertainment, and food. Add up how much money you spent under each category. Could you spend less money in one area and have more money for something else? What adjustments would you like to make next week?

5. Continue your money diary for a second week. At the end of the week, analyze the amounts you spent under each category again. Do you like what you did with your money better this week, or do you want to make more changes?

6. Keep the money diary a third week and analyze your spending. By the end of the third week, you should have a very good idea of your strengths and weaknesses with money. Some young people find this system so helpful, they decide to use it year round.

GOAL #4: TO REACH A SHORT-TERM SAVINGS GOAL

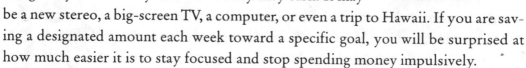

Most young entrepreneurs have many short-term goals for things they want to buy with the money they earn. It may be a new stereo, a big-screen TV, a computer, or even a trip to Hawaii. If you are saving a designated amount each week toward a specific goal, you will be surprised at how much easier it is to stay focused and stop spending money impulsively.

A monthly budget is a very useful tool for managing money. After you have kept a money diary for several weeks, it will be fairly easy to construct a monthly budget that includes saving for both short-term and long-term goals. A form for writing a budget was included in Chapter 7.

These are some other suggestions for staying on your budget:

Keep your goal in mind every day. Cut out pictures of the rollerblades you want to buy, and put them on your bulletin board or bathroom mirror. Think about the fun you will have when you reach your goal.

Track your savings with a chart. Measure weekly progress on a chart or bar graph. Each time you save, color in a little more of the bar to show how much closer you are to the goal.

Put your money in the bank. You won't be as tempted to spend the money if it's out of reach. Open a savings account and deposit your money each week. Remember, while your money is in the bank, it's earning more money (interest).

Stay out of the stores. Don't go shopping unless it's for things planned in your budget. Discipline yourself to wait. The rewards are worth it.

GOAL #5: TO SAVE TOWARD A LONG-TERM GOAL

A budget will also help you save for long-term goals such as college or your first car. Money that is being saved for long-term goals will multiply faster if you place it in a financial vehicle that pays higher interest. Examples of accounts that normally earn higher interest are certificates of deposit and mutual funds.

Ron Brown, owner of Another Dimension Mobile D.J. Service, sets yearly financial goals for his business. In addition to buying new sound equipment, Ron uses some of his money for daily expenses. He also pays a monthly car payment and car insurance. This year, Ron decided to designate part of his business income for long-term savings. After consulting with a financial planner, Ron chose to set aside $50 a month in a mutual fund.

The best person to advise you about long-term savings goals is a certified financial planner (CFP). You'll find CFPs who offer free consultations listed in your phone book. During your consultation, the financial planning expert will ask about your goals and discuss all your options for saving at the highest rates of return.

Don't be embarrassed to ask questions during your consultation. It takes everyone time to learn about investing. CFPs want to be sure their clients are informed and knowledgeable. Do your research, ask questions, then decide where to place your money.

A great book to read that tells how to save, spend, and invest money wisely is *How to Become a Teenage Millionaire*, by Todd Temple (Thomas Nelson Publishers, 1991).

GOAL #6: TO REINVEST MONEY BACK INTO THE BUSINESS

Smart entrepreneurs plan for ways to build the overall value of their business. Ron Brown advises young entrepreneurs to use the time while they are still living at home to build their business as fast as they can. Each time you reinvest more money into your business to buy equipment, supplies, inventory, or raw materials, you are increasing the worth of your business.

The value of your business is measured by this formula:

Assets - Liabilities = Net Worth

Assets include cash, equipment, tools, office supplies, materials, inventory, or anything else the business owns. *Liabilities* are any loans or bills the business owes. The special report business people use to calculate the total value of their business is a *balance sheet*.

On the next page (page 126) you will find a form to help you construct a balance sheet and determine the current worth of your business. It is very helpful to make balance sheets every few months, so you can see how the value of the business is growing.

GOAL #7: TO PREPARE FOR A CAREER

The path of entrepreneurship is one of the most exhilarating adventures a young person can pursue. Daryl Bernstein, 17-year-old author of *Better Than a Lemonade Stand*, a collection of 51 business ideas for kids, says, "Entrepreneurship is wildly exciting." He likes to set basic rules for his business but tries to remain open for every turn in the road. Daryl likes to "be ready to take short cuts, go off on detours, or stop and enjoy the scenery." He also compares business to a tromp through the jungle. "You've got to be ready to run from the lion, avoid the waterfalls, and navigate the rivers, if you want to make in business," states Daryl.

BALANCE SHEET

Company name: _____

_____

Date: _____

Assets:

Current Value:

Cash on hand: $ _____

Equipment: _____

Tools: _____

Supplies: _____

Raw materials: _____

Other: _____ _____

Other: _____ _____

Total assets: _____

Liabilities:

Bills owed: $ _____

_____

_____

_____

Loans: _____

_____

Total liabilities: _____

Net worth (assets–liabilities): _____

Daryl Bernstein wrote *Better Than a Lemonade Stand* (Beyond Words Publishing, 1992) when he was 15, and he's tried every business idea in the book. Currently, Daryl operates three businesses while attending his first year of college at Arizona State University. Logo Pro is a graphics design business that allows Daryl to do what he loves best: help other people start new businesses. Global Video is Daryl's educational video production and sales company. And Daryl Bernstein International is his consulting firm in which Daryl's main activities are writing, speaking, and providing business training. Daryl's most recent book is *Kids Can Succeed,* 51 tips on success from one kid to another, published in 1993 by Bob Adams, Inc.

About setting goals, Daryl says, "Income goals are a good place for kids to start. Money motivated me in the beginning. But now that I've made it, money doesn't motivate me any longer. I am in business because I love it."

Daryl is one of the many young entrepreneurs in this book who discovered a career while experimenting with business ideas. If you are interested in discovering a career, Daryl advises that you choose a business based on your interests or hobbies. Daryl says, "Do whatever it takes, but find a passion. Then do it well, and do it a lot."

The remainder of this book contains over 101 suggested businesses for young entrepreneurs. As you read through the next few chapters and select business ideas, remember to look for the passion. Don't be satisfied with money and material possessions alone. Look for ideas that are exciting, rewarding, and challenging. Look for ways to explore your talents and develop new strengths. Look for something you love so much, you'd be happy doing it the rest of your life. Loving what you do is the secret of success. I hope every young person who reads this book becomes wildly successful.

·9·

How to Make Money with a Service Business

If you need a business that costs almost nothing to start, this chapter is the place to look. Most of the businesses described here need only $5 to $20 in supplies to get started. There is no inventory to buy or product to manufacture. What you are selling is your time, knowledge, experience, and physical energy.

Some of the most popular service businesses for beginning entrepreneurs are house sitting, dog washing, running errands, and various cleaning jobs. More experienced entrepreneurs may organize closets or garages, repair bikes, provide child care, or deliver flyers for local business owners. You will find 14 service businesses described in this chapter.

If you enjoy helping others, have a strong sense of responsibility, and always take pride in doing your best, you will enjoy owning a service-based business.

Some of the advantages of a service business are:

1. Almost every young person has experience performing some type of household chore that can be marketed as a service business.

2. Service can be provided almost anywhere, anytime, for anyone. It's a business with unlimited potential.

3. Start-up is fast and requires very little cash.

4. It's flexible. You can set your own hours and work as little or as much as you want.

. . . SOMETHING YOU DO FOR OTHERS!

Some drawbacks of a service business are:

1. Sometimes service involves doing things no one likes to do. The work can occasionally be dirty, tiring, lonely, or just plain boring. Having a friend as a partner helps.

2. If you promise someone a job, you have to do it whether you feel like it or not. (But you'll feel better when you get paid.)

3. It's difficult to measure and price the worth of your work. Use a price list that's based on the going rate charged by similar businesses in your area.

THREE STEPS TO EXCELLENT CUSTOMER SERVICE

Step 1: Get a written agreement. Before you accept a job, show the customer your price list and discuss your pay. Then write your agreement on the order form provided in Chapter 6. Describe the work you are going to do, the amount you will be paid, and the date the job is to be completed. Ask for the customer's signature at the bottom. This may seem unnecessary at times, but if you follow this procedure you will have very few disagreements with customers.

Step 2: Under-promise and over-deliver. When setting dates to complete jobs for customers, always give yourself extra time for unexpected interruptions or delays. If your customer is not expecting his order for a week, you've "under-promised" what you can do. If you deliver it in 3 days, you've pleasantly surprised the customer by "over-delivering." Customers always appreciate a young entrepreneur who does a better job than expected.

Step 3: Make your customers your top priority. After you get the sale, do what you promised.

Provide top-quality service in a timely manner.

Do something extra without being asked.

Offer a guarantee or warranty on your service.

Express appreciation when you get paid.

Keep follow-up appointments faithfully.

Get in the habit of using an appointment calendar to schedule your work, and keep track of deadlines. Remember that your customers are your greatest asset. Being successful in a service business means becoming an expert at serving customers well.

START-UP #1: GO-FER DELIVERIES

It's easy to be a "go-fer." All you have to do is go-fer things when busy people don't have time to go-fer their own stuff. For example, your neighbor who is painting his garage might hire you to go-fer more paint brushes. A business owner might ask you to go-fer copies at the copy shop or pick up sandwiches for lunch.

Your main job as a go-fer is to take care of all your customers' errands and deliveries. You can be a general go-fer who is available pretty much anytime after school and on weekends. Or you can be a go-fer for special occasions.

Here's an example. On Super Bowl Sunday, Daryl Bernstein, author of *Better Than a Lemonade Stand*, organized a half-time delivery service for everyone having football parties on his block. A few minutes before half-time, Daryl and all his friends were waiting at the end of the street on their bikes. The moment half-time began, Daryl and his friends raced down the block, knocking on every door, saying, "Are you out of chips and dips or cold drinks? We're taking orders, and we'll go-fer whatever you need." Most people didn't want to take time away from their guests to go for supplies, so Daryl and his go-fer buddies made lots of money.

How to get started:

All sorts of people need go-fers. Your most regular clients will be small shops or offices within a few blocks of your house. Working moms and dads, older people, and handicapped persons also need your help. Get started by making flyers advertising your go-fer service. Then start asking your parents, neighbors, friends, their friends, their neighbors, and local business people. Soon you'll be the busiest go-fer in town!

START-UP #2: VACATION HOME CARE

Just before every holiday weekend, when people in your neighborhood are most likely to be planning a trip, pass out flyers announcing your house-sitting services. Jobs you can offer to do while they are gone are: get the mail, pick up newspapers, water plants, feed pets, exercise pets, mow the yard, shovel snow, inspect the house, take out trash, and call the owners if an emergency arises. Your neighbors will enjoy their vacation much more with someone dependable watching their property.

Suggestions for success:

1. Before accepting jobs, visit the home and get acquainted with the owners, pick up keys, get emergency numbers, and meet pets.

2. Make a list of all your duties and special instructions. Keep a daily checklist of your responsibilities and notes about what you did.

3. Be very careful when going in and out of the house. Double- and triple-check that doors are locked, windows closed, and gates shut. Never enter a house that looks like someone has broken in. Call the police and wait outside.

4. Do everything you promised. Then do something extra. Daryl Bernstein suggests leaving milk and donuts in the refrigerator with a note saying "welcome home."

Bonus idea: Barn sitter

People who raise animals often have a hard time going out of town because there is no one to care for their animals. If you have experience with farm animals or livestock, you can earn big bucks with a barn-sitting service.

START-UP #3: PROFESSIONAL ORGANIZER

Are you a person whose room is always neat? Do you keep drawers organized and know exactly what's on every shelf in your closet?

Use your talents to become a professional organizer. Messy people need your help organizing closets, cupboards, shelves, drawers, pantries, files, photo albums, record collections, clippings, recipes, children's rooms, garages, attics, basements, and storage rooms.

How to get started:

Make flyers or business cards advertising your services and rates. Since most people's possessions are very personal, your best customers will be folks you already know. Once you do a few jobs, word-of-mouth will bring you more business. For extra messy people, schedule monthly visits for touch-ups and repeats. Your customers will love you if you keep them organized!

YOU MESS IT UP—
WE CLEAN IT UP!

START-UP #4: IRONING SERVICE

Ironing is a time-consuming chore most busy people can't take time to do. Their only alternative is to take clothes that need ironing to a dry cleaners, which is fairly expensive. This spells opportunity for you.

All you need to start an ironing service is an iron, an ironing board, a spray bottle for water, spray starch, and a few flyers. Three or four regular customers will keep you busy and bring in $25 to $50 a week.

Tips for success:

Men's shirts will be your mainstay. Get new customers by offering a half-price special on shirts.

Avoid fabrics such as silk, linen, and wool. Stick with basic garments in cottons and cotton blends.

Check your iron frequently to make sure it's clean. If you need steam, a spray bottle of water is more reliable than a spray iron.

Each time the customer picks up ironing, ask when she or he is bringing the next bunch. Schedule jobs carefully so that every customer is satisfied and work is steady.

Bonus idea: Mending services

If you want to earn a little extra money, offer to sew on buttons, repair small rips in seams, or replace missing snaps and hooks. Your best marketing tool will be a price list showing all your ironing and mending fees.

START-UP #5: BIKE TUNEUP SERVICE

Sooner or later all bikes need to be fixed. Tires go flat. Spokes fall out. Seats wobble. For someone who knows how to do these jobs, the solutions are simple. But for most people, a broken bike is a major hassle. Save your neighbors time and money with a bike tune-up service.

How to get started:

1. Learn by watching other repair experts, reading books or manuals, and practicing on your own bike.

2. Gather basic tools and arrange space to work.

3. Use signs and flyers to make sure every bike owner in your area knows about you. Put a sign on your own bike when you go riding.

4. When you see a kid with bike trouble or a disabled bike in someone's yard, leave one of your flyers.

5. Make a price list to help with quick price quotes.

6. Keep some basic parts on hand, like bike tubes, master links, and spare pedals.

7. Offer a spring tune-up special for bikes that have been stored in garages all winter.

Bonus idea: Detailing service

Serious bikers take great pride in maintaining their bikes. Offer to wash, wax, and detail bikes for neighbors who want to look their best and keep their bikes operating at top performance.

START-UP #6: PARTY EXPERT

Everyone likes to be invited to a party! Here's your invitation to make money with a party service business.

Party services may include:

1. Shopping for party supplies

2. Cleaning and decorating the house

3. Preparing food; kitchen assistance

4. Taking coats, assisting guests, serving food, washing dishes, and leaving the hosts free to enjoy the guests

5. Offering to entertain children in another room

6. Afterwards, helping clean up

How to get started:

1. Learn all you can about party planning, food service, and decorating by reading books and magazines. Then improve your skills by helping at a few parties for free.

2. Local caterers often hire extra help for parties and events. This is a way to get paid while you learn more about your business.

3. Demonstrate your talents by helping at family events or holiday gatherings. Then pass out cards or flyers announcing your new business.

4. Most business comes from people seeing you work at other parties. Remember that every guest at this week's party is a potential customer for next week's event.

Bonus idea: Children's party planner

Busy parents need experts like you to plan parties for birthdays and holidays such as Halloween, Christmas, Kwanza, Valentine's Day, St. Patrick's Day, and Easter. You will find most of your customers through PTA meetings, day care centers, churches, synagogues, scouts, and 4-H. Use colorful flyers to advertise parties on various themes and give examples of your fees.

START-UP #7: PHOTOGRAPHY SERVICE

People love pictures of their kids, their pets, and themselves. Take photos at Christmas programs, school plays, dance recitals, parties, reunions, and sports events. If your camera develops film instantly, sell pictures on the spot. If not, get names and addresses, and go back later to sell the photos.

One young man made a business of attending weekend motocross races and photographing all the riders. The next weekend, everyone was back at the track to practice, and he was there again selling all the photos.

To photograph pets, you will need to visit pets at home. Take along some toys and props to make attractive pictures. Then frame the photos and sell them as gifts.

A book that will help you learn basic photography skills is *Photography: Take Your Best Shot*, by Terri Morgan and Shmuel Thaler (Lerner Publications).

START-UP #8: WHITE BIRD RELEASE

Brad Niles, age 17, of Los Gatos, California, owns a flock of 125 white homing pigeons. He helps people celebrate weddings, grand openings, and anniversaries by providing flocks of white birds displayed in decorated cages. The homing pigeons, which look a lot like doves, are a symbol of peace and unity. Brad charges $200 to attend a wedding (within 35 miles) and release 20 to 25 birds during the ceremony. The birds circle the party below, then fly home.

Brad's business is called Avian Joy. He and his sister, Amy, started raising homing pigeons almost 7 years ago when she was 13 and he was 10. Today Amy is in college studying to be a vet, and Brad runs the business.

Most of Brad's customers learn about Avian Joy through small ads in the local wedding guide magazine. He also attends bridal fairs and trade shows and is friends with lots of caterers and wedding consultants.

According to Brad, it takes about 30 minutes a day to feed and train the birds, which are housed in an aviary in their backyard. Brad cautions that only people who really love birds should try this business. If you are interested, the first step is to check zoning ordinances for restrictions that might apply. Amy says there are books in the library on how to raise homing pigeons, but the best place to learn about the birds is a homing pigeon club.

START-UP #9: VIDEO TAPING SERVICE

Everyone loves to see themselves on TV! If you have access to a video camera, you can make money filming dance recitals, school programs, birthday parties, holidays, family reunions, or almost any special event. People won't be able to resist buying a copy if they know their family is on the video.

Another service you can offer anytime of the year is a video inventory service. A local insurance agent will supply you with a list of items that should be inventoried in every home or business. Your video-taped record will help prove a claim if your customer ever has a loss.

To learn the basic techniques of video taping, read *How to Make Your Own Video*, by Perry Schwartz (Lerner Publications).

START-UP #10: BABYSITTER FINDER

Finding a sitter is always a problem for parents. They will be glad to pay you a small fee to find a good sitter.

How to get started:

1. Find out who babysits or wants to babysit in your neighborhood. Explain how you can help them get more jobs.

2. Make a 3 × 5 card for each sitter, showing his or her name, address, phone, age, experience, and hours available.

3. Ask sitters to provide at least three letters of reference from previous customers.

4. Go places where you will meet parents of young children. Hand out cards and flyers advertising your finder service throughout your neighborhood.

Tips for success:

Set a basic fee, but charge more for rush jobs.

Always start calling for a sitter as soon as you get a request. Fast service will influence parents to call again.

Require that sitters pay a small commission each time you get them a job.

Call parents the next day and see how things went. Drop sitters that don't do a good job. You only want to represent the best.

Bonus idea: Sitter directory

Another approach to this business is to publish a sitter directory. You can list both adult and teen sitters, as well as day care centers, mother's-day-out programs, and city recreational programs that provide drop-in sitting. Each sitter or business that wants to be in the directory should pay a small fee. You can also sell advertising space in the directory. Distribute the directories free or sell them for $1 to $2 each.

START-UP #11: AFTER-SCHOOL CHILD CARE

Lots of children come home from school to an empty house every day because their parents work. Since they often carry the key to their front door on a string around their neck, people call them *latchkey* children. Parents worry a lot about the safety of their latchkey children.

If you enjoy children and are a very responsible person, consider a business taking care of latchkey kids in your neighborhood. Ideally, you would walk the children home from school and stay with them until their parents get home. If you don't get out of school early enough to do that, you can go straight to their house after school. You may also get paid for extra services such as helping with homework, running a load of wash, or starting supper.

Another plan would be to offer several families a regular drop-in service. After school, you would have a route of several homes where you drop in and check on the kids, spend 30 minutes or so, then go to the next house. Wear a pager so kids can beep you if there is an emergency.

START-UP #12: SPECIAL AFTERNOONS

If you like kids, but would rather not babysit every afternoon, try offering two special afternoons a week when parents can send children to your house for stories, crafts, cooking lessons, exercise classes, puppet theater, or group playtime. Get new ideas for things to do from books at the library or by asking teachers you know.

Jimmy Gherdovich of Magnolia, Texas, had a business like this during the summer he was 13. Instead of special afternoons, however, Jimmy had a story time on Wednesday mornings. He advertised by passing out flyers. His fee was $2 per kid for 2 hours of stories, refreshments, and games. The moms enjoyed the time off, and the kids loved being entertained. Jimmy's mom, a teacher, was home in case there were any problems with the kids. Jimmy worked only 2 hours a week and made $4 to $6 an hour doing something he enjoyed.

START-UP #13: ELDERLY CARE SERVICE

Older people often have problems getting chores done around the house and yard. Taking heavy trash to the curb, getting things out of the attic, and sweeping the driveway are examples. You could be a real help by starting an elderly care service in your neighborhood.

How to get started:

1. Make flyers advertising your service, listing suggested chores, and telling about yourself and the hours you are available.

2. Some of the best places to find clients are churches and synagogues, senior citizen's centers, beauty shops, craft stores, and doctor's offices.

3. Before you accept a job, make an agreement in writing that states your hours, duties, and rate of pay.

4. Don't just do your chores and leave. Take time to get to know your older friends. They tell great stories and remember things you only read about in history books.

5. Look for extra services you can provide. You might cook a light meal, do laundry, or clean the bathtub. Some families may want you to call their elderly parent on the days you don't visit them in person.

6. Be dependable. Many elderly people are lonely and disabled. If you don't show up, they won't have anyone else to take your place. Train a backup person to do your job in case you are sick or out of town.

Bonus idea: Exercise partner

Older people often need help staying on a regular exercise program. Offer additional services as an exercise partner or "cheerleader" for the elderly. Exercising or taking walks is much more fun with a partner.

START-UP #14: FLYER DISTRIBUTOR

Business owners and political candidates often hire young people to deliver flyers and advertisements to the homes in your neighborhood. The best way to find jobs like this is to contact local advertising agencies, campaign chairpersons, or marketing consultants.

When Shannon Ramsey of Houston, Texas, was 16, she wanted to earn money to save for college. Her mother, who owns an advertising agency, had lots of clients who wanted handbills delivered. So Shannon filed a DBA and went into business for herself. The name of her business is Han-Del-Mail.

At first Shannon did all the delivery herself. She charged 6 cents per flyer, so the faster she walked, the more money she earned. Shannon found she could make an average of $7 per hour.

When Han-Del-Mail started getting clients like Pizza Hut and Century 21, Shannon had to hire workers to help. Since she had to pay workers 5 cents a flyer, Shannon increased her delivery price to 8 cents a flyer. Customers knew she did a good job, so they paid the extra to work with someone reliable.

For Shannon, delivery work is most profitable when she gets several clients who need flyers delivered in the same area on the same date. She pays her workers more to deliver three or four advertising pieces at once, but she makes a lot more for her time.

Shannon recommends that if you start a business like this, you never send people out to work without supervision. Here are some of her rules about flyer delivery:

1. Don't put flyers in mailboxes or throw them on driveways or sidewalks. They must be left on the doors.

2. Workers sometimes do things to get rid of flyers, such as leaving extras on doors, throwing flyers in the ditch, or scattering them in the streets. This cheats the client, angers the homeowners, and reflects poorly on your business. Insist that workers follow directions or quit.

3. If you get a complaint from your client or a homeowner, go out and investigate in person. If a complaint is valid, Shannon does the job over at no charge.

4. Hire young people who really need the money. They work harder, says Shannon. She had one young man who ran between houses and made $10 per hour.

5. Instruct workers to stay away from animals and skip vacant houses. For safety, Shannon usually has kids work in pairs, staying across the street from each other. Shannon drives and watches for any problems.

6. Shannon requires that small businesses pay in advance. When they bring her the flyers to be delivered, she verifies the number of flyers and gives them a bill. Some clients have been known to slip in extra flyers, thinking Shannon won't notice she is delivering the extras for free.

7. Learn to be firm, but assertive, about your prices and business practices. Clients and workers will respect your standards.

Shannon says that one of the greatest skills she has learned by owning a business like Han-Del-Mail is to be a diplomatic leader. She loves the flexible hours and challenge of being her own boss. Shannon, now 19, attends college on a debate scholarship, works 20 hours a week for her mom's advertising agency, and manages Han-Del-Mail.

·10·

HOW TO SPECIALIZE IN CLEANING THINGS

CLEANING IS A BOOMING BUSINESS. WHY? BECAUSE EVERYTHING GETS DIRTY. AND because more and more families have both mom and dad working, people don't have time to clean. This is an unlimited money-making opportunity for young entrepreneurs.

Advantages of a cleaning business:

1. Cleaning is in great demand. More people than ever are paying some-one to clean for them.

2. Cleaning is easy to learn. Practice at home—your parents will love it!

3. Cleaning can be done over and over. You can develop a list of regular customers.

4. A cleaning service is easy to expand. Just add new services as you see the needs of your customers growing.

5. Your service is also needed by local businesses, small shops, and offices. You can work anywhere.

Drawbacks of a cleaning business:

1. Some cleaning jobs may involve climbing ladders or using dangerous chemicals. It is against child labor laws for anyone under 18 to do this kind of work.

2. Most customers are very particular about how their cleaning is done. If you do a poor job, you'll have to do it over again. Avoid

disputes by setting high standards and being more particular than the customers are.

3. Cleaning is a boring activity for people who are artistic and social. Choose this business because you enjoy detail and like to make things look good, not just because it makes money. Money won't pat you on the back or tell you a joke when you're bored.

HOW TO USE NETWORKING TO FIND MORE CUSTOMERS

Shane had done some car-detailing jobs for neighbors, but he wanted more customers. He asked his dad if any of his friends needed car detailing. His dad asked people at work and found one good prospect. Shane asked for the job and got it. After that, Shane asked his aunt to watch for jobs and got several more customers. Finding work through friends and relatives is called *networking*.

Networking is a skill anyone can use. The first step is to figure out who is in your network or circle of contacts. Take a sheet of paper, draw a small circle in the center. That represents you.

Think of yourself as the center of a bull's-eye pattern. Draw a slightly larger circle around "you." Label this circle "family." Draw another circle around the bull's-eye of "you" and "family." Label it "friends." Then draw a fourth circle a little further out. In this circle, write "neighbors & acquaintances."

On another sheet of paper, write the names of all the people represented in each circle. Now go back to each name. Whom do they know who might need your service? Write the names of *their friends, family, and acquaintances*. All these people are part of your network.

If you know how to plug into your network, you should have no problem finding jobs. These are some smart networking strategies:

1. Get out and talk to people in your network. The more people you tell about your business, the more people you ask for leads, the more likely you are to find new customers.

2. Start with the circle of contacts closest to you: your family. Contact casual acquaintances last.

3. Follow up on every contact and every lead you get. Keep names and phone numbers. Explore every possibility.

4. Ask previous customers if they know anyone who needs your service. A referral from a satisfied customer is the most valuable network contact you can receive.

5. Build your network by sharing leads you don't use with your friends. Always show appreciation to those who help you.

This chapter contains outlines for 16 different cleaning businesses appropriate for young entrepreneurs. Once you find customers, here's how to get even more referrals: Keep your customers happy.

SEVEN WAYS TO KEEP CUSTOMERS HAPPY

1. Be cheerful and courteous. Show you are interested in doing good work. Discuss the job and the pay before you start.

2. Dress neatly and be on time. Customers appreciate dependability.

3. Make a detailed list of instructions and check off each step as it is completed.

4. Be careful with cleaning solutions, and don't damage property in any way. If an accident happens, report it immediately and offer to pay for damages.

5. Don't be distracted by TV, kids, friends, or pets. Work steadily. Listening to music sometimes helps you work better. But don't annoy customers with your music. Use earphones.

6. Clean up after your job, put back anything you moved, and haul away all trash.

7. Always say thanks when you get paid, and set an appointment for the next time.

START-UP #15: TRASH CAN PATROL

Taking out the trash is one of those jobs everyone hates to do. A smart young entrepreneur can turn trash into a gold mine.

How to get started:

1. Make some flyers advertising your Trash Can Patrol. List such services as taking cans to the curb, returning cans to the house, or setting out things for recycling pickups.

2. Also offer inside trash services. With this service, the night before trash pickup, you go to the house, empty all the household cans, and prepare the trash for the next day.

3. Set rates for all your services. Some young people charge $5 a month for two trash pickups a week. That averages out to about 25 cents each time you take a can in or out.

4. Be energetic and confident when you go knocking on doors and handing out your flyers. Offer free service for a week. This will give you time to demonstrate your dependability and prove the value of your service.

Additional services for a trash can patrol:

Recycling services

Washing and deodorizing wastebaskets and cans

Painting house numbers or last names on cans

Two boys named Ashley and Karsten started a trash-toting business in the apartment complex where they lived. They noticed that their neighbors hated carrying trash downstairs and across the parking lot to the trash bin every morning. So Ashley and Karsten offered to do the job.

Ashley and Karsten set up a regular route of trash pickup customers. Then they took turns running the route before school every morning. Each neighbor paid them 50 cents for every trip they made to the dumpster.

START-UP #16: CLEANING TECHNICIAN

How fast can you clean a house? Today's house-cleaning specialists are experts at thorough, yet fast, service. Male or female, they clean a whole house in about 3 hours.

Before you advertise yourself as a cleaning technician, try it at home, and be sure you can do the work. If you can, you will make good money. Average pay runs between $5 and $10 an hour.

Services to offer:

Sweeping or vacuuming all floors

Dusting the whole house

Mopping the kitchen and bathroom

Cleaning all sinks, toilets, tubs, and showers

Washing kitchen tables and countertops

Changing bed linens

This is what is called a *general house cleaning*. Spring cleanings or deep cleanings are extra. Examples of extra services are: cleaning ceiling fans, doing laundry, washing walls or woodwork, cleaning the oven and refrigerator, or polishing furniture. Clients should provide all equipment and cleaning products, as well as detailed instructions.

START-UP #17: SHOE AND BOOT SERVICE

People who like to be well groomed need clean and polished shoes. If you knock on their door offering to pick up scuffed and dirty shoes and return them the next day clean and shiny, you'll probably find lots of people saying Yes.

Take a before-and-after example with you when you go out to sell. Show one shoe before it was polished and another shoe after it was polished. Then give customers your rate sheet and ask what day is best to pick up their shoes.

For extra income, offer additional services such as cleaning golf shoes, running shoes, riding boots, work boots, dress boots, and sneakers. Set your rates so you average at least $4 to $5 an hour.

START-UP #18: KITCHEN SPECIALIST

The average homeowner seldom has time to do a really thorough cleaning in the kitchen. Yet the kitchen can be the dirtiest spot in the house. After a while, grease and spills build up, and the job is an all-day affair. It should easily be worth $50 to $100 to have an energetic cleaning specialist take care of the problem. This would also be a great business for a team, with each member specializing in a particular area of the kitchen.

What your detailing job may include:

Washing the fronts of all cabinets

Applying furniture oil to wood cabinets

Detailed cleaning of stove top, oven, and microwave

Cleaning toasters and coffeemakers

Cleaning all countertops and sinks and removing stains

Using a soft cloth and toothbrush to clean the door on the dishwasher

Cleaning out the refrigerator

Using appliance cleaner on the exterior of the refrigerator

Sweeping the floor

Mopping the floor and cleaning baseboards

Cleaning fingerprints around light switches and doors

If you don't have an entire Saturday to spend on one customer's kitchen, arrange to do the job on two afternoons after school. Always ask satisfied customers for names of friends who might want the same service.

START-UP #19: BATHROOMS ARE OUR ONLY JOB

Cleaning bathrooms is the chore homeowners say they dislike the most. However, once a bathroom is well cleaned the first time, weekly touch-ups are very easy.

If you plan to specialize in bathrooms, charge a higher rate for first-time cleaning. Then set up a schedule to make weekly house calls.

Bonus idea: Business restrooms

Public restrooms in small businesses, shops, and offices need to be cleaned at least once a day. Visit business establishments in your community, and offer bathroom-cleaning services daily or every other day. Remember, business restrooms don't have tubs and showers, so they are even easier to clean.

If you charge $3 per visit and take 30 minutes to do the job, you'll be earning about $6 an hour. Cleaning one bathroom five times a week will bring in $15, but most businesses have two bathrooms. You could earn $30 a week cleaning two bathrooms for only one customer.

START-UP #20: WINDOW-WASHING TECHNICIAN

There are lots of people with dirty windows in your neighborhood. They're just waiting for someone like you to save them from having to do the job. Give yourself the title of window-washing technician.

How to get started:

1. First become an expert. Practice on your own windows at home until you have developed a good system for cleaning windows.

2. Prepare to mobilize. Fix up a box or bucket with all your supplies for washing windows. Decide how much you will charge, and start looking for customers.

3. Pass out flyers advertising your window-washing service to everyone you know. Wait a few days. Then call each person back to ask if she or he is ready to have the windows cleaned.

4. Remember the best way to get more business is when your satisfied customers tell their friends and neighbors about your work. Always give each customer first-class service.

You can do twice as many jobs if you have a partner. One of you can work inside and the other outside. Keep a list of your customers, and call them again in 6 months. Their windows will be dirty again.

Bonus idea: Storm cleanup

If you have frequent dust storms, call your customers after every bad storm to see if they need window-washing services.

When a hurricane threatens coastal areas, homeowners are always advised to tape their windows. The tape is very difficult to remove once the storm has passed. One enterprising middle school student made a complete business out of removing tape from windows after hurricanes.

START-UP #21: POOL MAINTENANCE

If you have a pool and have learned to do the maintenance chores, you have a ready-made money-making skill. Two or three regular customers will give you spending money all summer.

How to get started:

1. If you don't own a pool, learn to do pool maintenance by working with a friend who does.

2. Get customers by giving out flyers, asking people who have pools, or putting small ads in the newspaper.

3. Before accepting a job, visit the home to see the pool, get instructions, and discuss how you will be paid.

4. Your goal should be to get a list of regular customers. Then keep a schedule and do each job at the same time each week.

5. Offer customers a price break if they will sign a contract for the whole summer season.

6. Be dependable, and your happy customers will tell others about you.

Pool-cleaning steps:

1. Test the water.

2. Add the chemicals.

3. Vacuum the pool.

4. Use a deep net to clean floating trash.

5. Use a skimmer net to clean the top of the water.

6. Check and clean the filter. Then backwash.

7. Brush the floor and sides of the pool.

8. Sweep and hose off decks and surrounding pool areas.

Almost any business that sells pool supplies has books and pamphlets on pool cleaning and maintenance. If you have any problems with a pool, these people are excellent resources.

Watching the profits:

Suppose you run a pool-cleaning service and make $125 profit in June and $175 profit in July. At first glance, it appears you made the most profit in July. However, you don't know this for sure until you look at the number of hours you worked each month.

This is the formula for figuring hourly wage:

$$\frac{\text{Profit}}{\text{Total Hours}} = \text{Hourly Wage}$$

If you worked 25 hours to make $125 in June, you earned $5 per hour. If you worked 40 hours to make $175 in July, you earned only $4.38 per hour. Now which month was most profitable? The real story on your profits is the amount you made per hour.

To keep track of how much you are earning per hour, write the amount of time you worked on each customer's receipt. At the end of the month, add up your time and figure your hourly wage. This system works for any service business.

START-UP #22: POWER WASHING SERVICE

When Hill Norvell was in tenth grade, he worked for a painting contractor in his spare time. Hill noticed that many times after the outside of a house was cleaned to prepare it for painting, it didn't really need to be painted. He decided to start his own business cleaning home exteriors.

Hill used $1,000 he had inherited from his grandmother to buy a high-powered pressure washing machine that sends a forceful spray of bleach and water onto the surface of the house and removes mildew, dirt, and loose paint. Then he started passing out flyers announcing his service. After a few jobs, most of his business came by word-of-mouth.

Today Hill owns a new Toyota truck he bought with the money he earned. He has graduated from high school and is attending Baylor University in Waco, Texas. His goal is to get a degree in marketing. He still runs his power-washing business and has added additional services that include cleaning patios, decks, pool areas, sidewalks, and driveways.

Is there a way to start this business without $1000? Rent a pressure washer for the first few months, then invest money in equipment. Before you buy new, check newspaper classified ads for used pressure washers.

START-UP #23: BOAT AND RV CLEANING

Millions of people in the United States own recreational vehicles (RVs). Stop right now and make a list of everyone you know who owns a boat, RV, small airplane, camp trailer, golf cart, dirt bike, or four-wheeler. Then think about all the people *they* know who own the same equipment.

What does all this mean to you? It means you may have access to hundreds of customers who need their recreational vehicles cleaned many times a year. This is your opportunity to earn big bucks.

How to get started:

1. Learn more about cleaning recreational vehicles by offering to help your friend clean his boat, airplane, or RV the next time it gets dirty. Don't charge anything. Just ask questions and pay attention to details.

2. Visit RV and boat dealerships and talk to the salespeople. They will have lots of information about maintenance. They may also need someone to clean the boats and RVs they have on display. You can learn even more by working for them.

3. Make some attractive flyers advertising your services and rates. Then pass them out wherever you see boats, RVs, planes, or dirt bikes. Dealerships may let you put flyers on their counters. Other good places to market are marinas, fishing piers, RV parks, golf courses, sporting equipment stores, and restaurants near recreational areas.

START-UP #24: COMPLETE CAR WASH

Washing cars to earn money is almost as traditional as having a lemonade stand. While it may not seem particularly exciting or new, it has withstood the test of time because it truly is a great way to earn money.

Here are some ways to improve the car-washing business today:

1. People today want their high-priced cars to be babied and pampered. Emphasize the fact that you hand-wash every car with mild soap and soft rags.

2. Many business people use their cars to transport clients or business associates. Their cars must be immaculately groomed. Emphasize your careful attention to making the inside and outside of the car spotless. Offer waxing and detailing at additional prices.

3. People today have less time. If you live near an office building, school, or shopping center, market a "car wash express" to

employees. Get a few friends to help you develop a precision plan for team washing a car in 15 minutes. Then set appointments and guarantee regular customers: "Your car spotless in 15 minutes or the car wash is free." Be sure to add a qualifier at the bottom of your flyer stating that your guarantee does not apply to first-time customers. Offer a first-time special also.

Although customers today expect a better car wash, the good news is they expect to pay a higher price. Check prices on hand washing and detailing in your area. Then see if you can gain the competitive advantage by giving just a little bit more service for a slightly lower price.

START-UP #25: GARAGE-CLEANING EXPERT

No matter how hard people try, garages get dirty, messy, and cluttered. If you are good at organizing things, make dirty garages your specialty. Garages are not hard to keep orderly if they are cleaned once a month.

How to do the job:

1. First throw away everything you know is trash.
2. Ask for a list of other things to throw away. Or put things you think can be thrown away in a box so that the customer can inspect it.
3. Then start removing things from shelves, washing shelves, and organizing contents into groups: things for the pool, things for the yard, things for painting, etc.
4. Make labels for shelves, and return items to shelves in logical order.
5. Move large items and sweep the floor. Charge extra for cleaning oil spots or pet areas.
6. Arrange large items in the garage neatly, and ask the owner to inspect the job.

Additional services you can offer are hosing and scrubbing the floor, painting, building simple shelves, or hauling off discards. Some young people make extra money selling items they are given when they clean a garage.

START-UP #26: COMMERCIAL CLEANING

Owners of small businesses often have to do their own cleaning. But if the business is growing, the owner will soon need a cleaning service. Most cleaning services have overhead expenses to run their offices and pay for advertising. You can undercut their rates and offer the same services.

Some customers will only need your help at busy times of the year. Others will want you to come on a regular schedule. Your work will usually be done after the business closes while the owner is doing bookkeeping or paperwork.

Suggestions for success:

1. Work with the business owner to make a checklist of your duties. Then use the checklist as a reminder list every time you work. Your most likely duties will be vacuuming or sweeping, dusting, mopping, cleaning display cases, emptying trash, and disinfecting bathrooms.

2. You may also want to offer parking lot maintenance services, lawn care, or daily window-washing services. Your jobs and rate of pay should be stated in a written agreement signed by your customer.

3. Watch for vacant houses or apartments with "For Rent" signs. Call the number on the sign and offer services for rental property cleaning. Don't quote a price until you see the inside. Renters often leave a place trashed out.

START-UP #27: FISH AQUARIUM SERVICE

Research proves that watching fish swim around in aquariums helps people relax and relieves stress. That's why so many dentists, doctors, lawyers, and car dealers are putting aquariums in their waiting areas. However, the weekly maintenance required on an aquarium can add more stress to business owners.

If you enjoy fish, make it your mission to become an expert in aquarium maintenance. Most aquarium experts specialize in either salt-water or freshwater environments. Average pay for this service is well over $10 an hour.

START-UP #28: PET-GROOMING TECHNICIAN

Most people feel that their pet is a member of the family. The pet stays inside, has a special bed, gets special food, sits in everyone's lap, and is part of every family occasion. Keeping a pet clean is a necessity. However, it is a very time-consuming job, even if you take the pet to a groomer.

The newest trend in pet grooming is the mobile service. Instead of the pet being taken to the groomer, the groomer comes to the pet. Usually this mobile service is offered in a custom van outfitted for pet grooming.

You may not have money to buy a grooming van, but you can still save pet owners time and money. Offer your services as a pet-grooming technician who makes weekly house calls to give pets baths and flea treatments.

Bonus idea: Training services

If you have had experience training animals, you have another marketable skill. Offer your customers the added service of obedience training or show training.

START-UP #29: CAGE AND STALL CLEANING

Christy Hurlburt of Englewood, Colorado, has loved riding horses since she was 9 years old. Last year when she was 15, her parents agreed to buy her a horse, if she would pay for its room and board. That meant Christy had to earn money.

First she made arrangements with a friend who owned a two-horse barn. Christy promised to keep the barn clean on a weekly basis, if her horse could stay in the extra stall for free. Then Christy started a business she calls Christy's Muck and Feed.

Christy knows lots of people with horses. Whenever anyone goes out of town or is too busy to care for their animals, they call Christy. She mucks (cleans) stalls and feeds, grooms, and exercises horses. Typical fees are $10 a day for muck and feed and $10 an hour for exercising the horse.

Another part of Christy's business is giving English riding lessons, for which she charges $15 an hour. Christy feels she is a very lucky person to be able to work outdoors with the animals she loves.

Getting started:

If you love animals, find a way to get paid to be around them. One way is to clean cages for birds, hamsters, gerbils, rabbits, chickens, and ducks. Or specialize in cleaning stalls and sheds for farm animals like sheep, goats, and horses.

Advertise your services with flyers left at pet stores, feed stores, stables, and veterinarian's offices. Participate in 4-H and take agricultural classes at school. Every time you meet another animal owner, you are meeting a potential customer.

START-UP #30: DOGGIE DOO CLEANUP SERVICE

I heard about this business several years ago and laughed at the very idea of someone getting paid to be a "pooper scooper." Today I'm reading articles in newspapers about real businesses making $40,000 a year for providing this very service.

One business I read about is Dog Butler, started by Richard Scott in Seattle, Washington, when he was 24 years old. In 1993 he had four employees picking up waste from 500 dogs weekly at 160 homes and kennels. He charges about $22 per month for weekly pickups. Each additional dog is $2 extra.

People give him funny nicknames like "The Poop Man" and "The Dog Doo Guy," but he laughs all the way to the bank.

If you've got a sense of humor this might be the business for you.

·11·

HOW TO MAKE MONEY WITH YARD AND GARDEN WORK

RESEARCHERS SAY THAT ALMOST HALF OF ALL THE KIDS WHO EARN MONEY GET STARTED by cutting grass or doing some type of yard work. If you would rather work outdoors than indoors, like to work with plants, and enjoy making a yard look its best, a lawn care business may be an excellent opportunity for you. This chapter contains 12 business ideas that involve yard and garden work or outdoor painting.

Why so many young people start yard and garden businesses:

1. Most kids learn how to do yard work at home. It's one of their best marketable skills.

2. Most families own mowers and lawn equipment. Young people can usually borrow equipment from mom and dad to get started.

3. Every home requires yard and garden maintenance. If you do good work, your services will be in great demand.

4. The amount of money you can earn is only limited by your time and physical energy.

Difficulties in yard and garden work:

1. Yard work is not just "kid work" any more. You will be competing against adults who have chosen lawn care as a profession. Your customers will expect a higher standard of performance.

2. Since most yard work is seasonal, it takes some planning to have a steady income. Choose a name that tells customers

you are a year-round service (*Example*: All Seasons Lawn Service). As each season approaches, give out new flyers that emphasize services for that time of year. The painting services recommended in this chapter can also be combined with seasonal yard work to produce a year-round income.

3. Yard work is a dirty job. If you can't handle the physical stress, find another way to be involved in this business. Consider becoming a booking agent for kids who like yard work but don't like sales. You do the marketing, get the jobs, assign the work, deal with customers, inspect work, and keep the records. They do the yards. Your share of the income should be 15% to 20%.

HOW TO USE FREEBIES TO GET MORE CUSTOMERS

Lots of businesses use free offers to get your attention. Buy a hamburger; get one free. Free movie rental if you rent six. Free car wash with fill-up.

David wanted to start a lawn care business a few summers ago. He watched how other businesses got new customers by offering things free. He decided this was a technique he could use also.

He noticed that one older lady on his block lived alone, had no children, and had no one to do her yard work. One afternoon when she was gone, David went to her house with his lawnmower. He mowed her yard, trimmed the hedges, swept the sidewalks, and left a note on her front door. The note said, "I mowed your yard for free. If you like the job I did, call me. I charge $20 a week."

Did he get the job? You bet he did.

This lady turned out to be one of his best customers. While David was in eleventh and twelfth grade, he mowed her yard about 20 times a year. If you multiply by $20, you'll see that David made $400 each year.

Was it worth giving away something worth $20 to earn $800? The answer is obviously, Yes.

LAWN AND GARDEN SAFETY

1. Wear sturdy work shoes to protect your feet and safety glasses to protect your eyes.

2. Protect your skin by wearing a hat, gloves, long sleeves, and long pants. Use sunscreen and insect repellant as necessary.

3. Don't enter yards with pets unless the owner is present.

    Avoid wasps, ants, and other insects.

4. Keep children and pets away from work areas.

5. Before mowing, inspect the yard. Pick up trash, rocks, wire, sticks, cans, and any other dangerous objects.

6. Never mow a wet lawn. It's bad for the grass, and your feet are more likely to slip under the mower.

7. Know your equipment and how to operate it safely.

8. To unclog or adjust the mower, turn it off and wait for the blade to stop.

9. Turn off and cool the mower before refueling. Refuel outside, not in the garage where gasoline vapors could be ignited by sparks from appliances.

10. Keep your equipment in good repair.

START-UP 31: LAWN CARE TECHNICIAN

Young people who do yard care today are competing with professional lawn care services. You can no longer think of yourself as a kid cutting grass. You must become a lawn care technician.

These are some ways to be more professional:

1. Get serious about learning to be an expert in lawn care. Observe other professionals. Read. Ask questions.

2. Make it your goal to do more than cut grass. Professionals take pride in grooming the whole lawn.

YOU GROW IT!
WE MOW IT!

TOM'S MOWING SERVICE
Call 973-2343

3. Keep your mower in good repair, so you get a smooth, even cut that looks like a carpet.

4. Always sweep sidewalks and driveways. Hand-pull grass around trees and shrubs.

5. Offer additional services such as edging, trimming, weeding, raking, or sweeping gutters.

6. Dress well and use advertising that looks professional.

If you offer high-quality service at lower prices than your competition, you will have plenty of customers.

Make it your goal to develop a list of regular weekly customers. Don't forget about business property. Check with local churches, banks, and shops. These jobs are usually bigger and pay more.

These are some marketing tools you will need:

A contract: Give customers a price break when they sign a monthly contract.

Business cards: Leave extra business cards with your customers so they can pass them along to friends.

T-shirts: Wear a T-shirt or jacket with your business name and phone number. People passing by may see it and want to hire you.

Success story: Matt & Shawn's Do It All Business

When Matt Hayden's older sister, Kelly, started a business making greeting cards, Matt was very impressed with all the money she was making. Matt decided right away that he wanted to start a business, too.

Taking stock of his assets and talents, Matt decided a lawn care business was his quickest way to wealth. He enlisted his best friend, Shawn Leuchuga, as a partner.

First, the two fourth-grade boys passed out flyers all over the neighborhood advertising Matt & Shawn's Do It All Business. On the flyer, they listed jobs they would do, such as mowing lawns, raking, weeding, snow shoveling, or pet sitting. By the summer, Matt and Shawn were averaging $30 a week income with about five regular customers.

Matt's advice for other kids who want to start a lawn care business is to learn how to be nice to customers. He attended a class at Young Americans Bank that taught him these steps to approaching customers:

1. First tell customers the name of your business, and hand them a business card.

2. Then introduce yourself and tell where you live. Letting your customer know that you are a neighbor builds trust.

3. Briefly explain the services you provide and ask, "Is there anything you need us to do today?"

4. If customers say No, don't be pushy. Invite them to call you in the future, and thank them as you leave.

The other advice Matt offers is "Learn to do the job correctly." He says he mowed his own yard at least 20 times before he was sure he could do someone else's yard for pay.

START-UP #32: LANDSCAPE ARTIST

Landscaping is not yard cutting or weeding. It is caring for shrubs, plants, and flowers in the yard. And it's deciding where shrubs, plants, and flowers would look best, preparing the soil, and planting them in the yard.

Good landscaping is an art. Plants of all sizes, shapes, and colors are the artist's tools to create a beautiful environment. You will enjoy this business if you enjoy gardening and enjoy being creative.

How to get started:

1. First, learn all you can about landscaping. The library has lots of books on the subject. If possible, take a class at school or at a local community center.

2. Spend several hours a week visiting local nurseries, studying the plants, asking questions, and learning what grows best in your climate. Nurseries usually have a wide selection of books on landscaping. Invest in one or two of the best books you can afford.

3. Talk to people you know who have well-landscaped homes. Ask how they made their decisions about plants and what kind of maintenance is required.

4. If you don't feel comfortable calling yourself a landscaper yet, advertise your services as an assistant

gardener. Then you can learn by helping more experienced gardeners construct beds, install borders, plant shrubs and flowers, mulch, water, trim, and prune.

5. Gradually start advertising more and more landscaping services in your business. First offer plant care such as trimming, mulching, and watering. Then add constructing beds and planting shrubs and flowers. Last, add selecting plants, designing beds, and placing trees and shrubs.

START-UP #33: STARTER PLANTS

People love to see their flower beds and gardens come alive after a long, cold winter. The best time to sell starter plants is in the spring. However, serious gardeners usually buy plants all year long.

How to get started:

1. If you are going to be a grower or supplier of starter plants, you will need to be very knowledgeable about what plants grow best in your climate. You can find out by visiting nurseries, asking other gardeners, or talking to your county extension or 4-H agent.

2. You will get the starter plants by growing them from seed, taking cuttings from other plants, or by getting thinnings from other gardeners. Most people hate to throw away good plants when they prune or thin, so they won't mind giving them to you. Houseplants, berry plants, and herbs are most commonly raised from cuttings.

3. If you are growing from seed, you need to plant about 6 weeks before planting season. Grow the plants in small paper cups or egg cartons filled with potting soil.

4. When the season starts, watch local prices closely. Since you have almost no expenses, you will be able to sell your plants for slightly less than other suppliers.

5. Watch for opportunities to earn additional money by doing the actual planting.

If you want to learn more about raising and selling herbs and produce in your own backyard, read *Pay Dirt* by Mimi Luebbermann (Prima Publishing).

START-UP #34: FRESH FLOWERS

Office workers and business people enjoy having fresh flowers on their desk. If you have room in your backyard, get permission to plant beds of flowers. Then sell the flowers in your own "flower of the week" club.

Members of the club would pay $10 to join and $2 a week. They will receive a nice vase that's theirs to keep, and you will deliver a different fresh flower each week for 3 months. At the end of each 3 months, they can again subscribe to your service.

Suggestions for success

1. In order to deliver a different flower each week, plant at least 12 varieties of flowers.

2. To start your service, you will need to have flowers ready to pick, or you will need a place to buy flowers wholesale until you can grow your own.

3. Flowers look bare without some greenery. Use part of one bed to grow some ferns and baby's-breath to make simple backings for the flower of the week.

4. Besides marketing your flowers through the flower-of-the-week club, you can also sell flowers to friends and neighbors for Valentine's Day, Mother's Day, anniversaries, birthdays, and other special occasions. Start taking orders about 2 weeks before each holiday.

START-UP #35: FRESH PRODUCE

Seventeen-year-old James Sharp, of Sims, North Carolina, has been growing and selling fresh produce for nearly 7 years. He started at age 10, growing a row of watermelons and cantaloupes. That year he made about $150 selling what the family didn't use to friends and relatives.

James enjoys growing things, so each year he has just kept increasing the length and number of rows. At age 13, he grew enough melons to supply one grocery store for the month of July, and earned about $500. At age 14, he increased his planting to half an acre and supplied two grocery stores. However, James never actually started calling his work a business until he was 15.

That year he planted 2 1/2 acres and registered his business name, Fresh-Pik Produce. He also had business cards printed and stickers made to put on the boxes of melons, tomatoes, lima beans, and peas he supplied to three stores. At this point, James said, "I enjoyed it so much, I knew I wanted to do produce farming the rest of my life."

James saved all the money he made selling produce, working on his dad's farm, and winning 4-H livestock shows. The year he turned 16, James made some investments toward his dream. First, he built a large greenhouse, so he could grow his own starter plants. Then he rented 10 acres from his parents. Next, he rented a tractor and bought a sprayer, planter, and plow. From the planting that year, James supplied eight local stores and had leftovers to sell to the wholesalers.

After James graduates from high school, he plans to attend North Carolina State University and major in horticulture. James knows he hasn't always made all the right decisions in his business, but overall he's been tremendously successful. His advice for other young entrepreneurs is, "Don't be afraid to make decisions for yourself. If it's wrong, you'll know how to do it right the next time."

START-UP #36: LEAF REMOVAL

In the fall, yard mowing gradually comes to an end and leaf raking begins. Study the chart below to see how much you can earn with this business.

POSSIBLE WEEKLY INCOME FROM RAKING LEAVES

Earning per yard	1 yard	2 yards	3 yards	4 yards
$5 once a week:	$5	$10	$15	$20
$5 twice a week:	$10	$20	$30	$40
$10 once a week:	$10	$20	$30	$40
$10 twice a week:	$20	$40	$60	$80

Figuring that the average leaf-raking season lasts 6 weeks, multiply each amount on the chart by 6. With several regular customers, you could "rake in" $30 to $480 before Christmas.

Any time of the year that you have severe weather such as a damaging wind storm, hail storm, or hurricane, you will have lots of chances to earn more money raking. Yards will be full of leaves, small twigs, limbs, and debris that must be removed. But you'll have to work fast. This is a limited-time opportunity.

Bonus idea: Selling mulch

Don't throw away those bags of leaves you rake in the fall.

Somebody will buy them to mulch their garden for the winter. Gardeners love mulch because it helps control weeds, enriches the soil, and holds in moisture. Other types of mulch they will buy are pine straw, hay, and ground bark.

START-UP #37: SNOW REMOVAL

In the winter the most profitable outdoor work for young people is snow removal. With a list of regular customers, you can earn good money in bad weather.

To get started you need warm clothes, a good snow shovel, and an ice scraper. Then team up with a hard-working friend and see how much you can earn.

Ways to get customers:

1. Pass out flyers announcing your snow-removal service throughout your neighborhood. Then go back to sign up regular customers who will agree to let you do all their snow removal.

2. For extra jobs, visit small businesses in your area early in the morning after a snow, and see if they need help.

3. If a customer is happy with your work, ask her or him to recommend you to a friend.

4. Don't forget your snow-removal customers after winter is over. Contact them when you are helping with gardens in the spring or mowing yards in the summer.

START-UP #38: FIREWOOD BUSINESS

City folks with fireplaces often have to pay high prices for their firewood. You can get firewood free and sell it in your neighborhood.

Sources of free firewood:

>Where land is being cleared
>
>Abandoned trees in the woods
>
>When a storm blows down trees or large limbs
>
>A neighbor who has a tree cut down or heavily pruned

Things you need to know about selling firewood:

1. Firewood is priced by cubic feet, which means a stack of wood 12 inches high, 12 inches long, and 12 inches wide.

2. Hardwoods sell for higher prices than softer woods. Soft woods are pine and firs. Oak or elm are harder. Fruit tree woods are the hardest.

3. Sell only what you can deliver with a wagon. Or find an adult as a partner who can help with transportation.

4. Make flyers to announce your service, and put them out all around your community. Go door-to-door and offer to supply firewood once a week throughout the winter.

5. When you're out gathering wood, make bundles of kindling out of small twigs and branches. It's easy to carry these along as you sell door-to-door.

6. Gather pinecones for firestarters. Melt old candles and dip the pinecones. Tell customers they make beautiful sparks and colors in the fire.

Bonus idea: Selling by the cord

When Daniel Dean of Magnolia, Texas, was 15, he knew some places to get free firewood, so he started selling firewood on the side of the highway near his home. Instead of selling by the cubic foot, Daniel sold wood by the cord. A cord of wood is 4 feet by 4 feet by 8 feet, or 128 cubic feet. Daniel made $135 for a full cord, delivered and stacked, or $75 for a half cord, delivered and stacked.

From this experience, Daniel's interest in timberland grew. He started following logging crews when he saw them go into the woods to work, just so he could watch and ask questions. During his senior year in high school, Daniel started the business he has today, Daniel Dean Timber Co.

This year, 20-year-old Daniel had billboards placed on the highways that say "Timber Wanted, Call 356-DEAN." He keeps four or five logging crews working most of the time, and he's building a reputation as an honest business person in his community. Daniel says the key to success is to "Always look people in the eye and tell the truth. That way you won't have to worry if you can't remember what you told them."

START-UP #39: WATERING SERVICE

People who spend a lot of money on their yards and outdoor plants, spend a lot of time watering. It is particularly important to water regularly in dry climates or during hot weather.

Getting started:

1. Your most likely customers for a watering service are busy families whose both parents work. Pass out flyers in your neighborhood during dry seasons of the year.

2. Pay close attention to vacation times, and advertise your services when families are most likely to be taking trips. Watering every day while they're gone could earn you a nice sum.

3. Have labels printed with your advertising message. Put them on plastic spray bottles and give them away free to your favorite customers. Every time they use the sprayer to mist a houseplant, they'll be reminded of your watering service.

Steps to success:

1. Always make lists of exact instructions for watering.

2. Find out how to locate the hoses, sprinklers, and any other equipment you will need.

3. Ask if there are other jobs you can do to help while they are out of town.

START-UP #40: OUTDOOR PAINTING

Outdoor painting is a great way beginning painters can learn to paint without much risk. Typical jobs you can offer to do are painting outdoor furniture, fences, dog houses, porches, decks, or storage sheds.

How to get started:

1. Take a good look around your neighborhood. Make note of possible target customers and specific projects.

2. Print some announcements of your painting service. Then visit each target customer on your list.

3. Make an agreement on the job to be done, the amount you will be paid, and who buys the supplies.

Tips for success:

Wear old clothes, shoes, and hat.

Keep all your paint rags, brushes, paint scraper, roller, and tools in one box or bucket.

Protect the area where you work from drips and spills with newspaper or drop cloths.

Remove loose paint, dirt, and grease before you paint.

Use a sturdy paint brush, and paint from top to bottom.

Clean up your mess, and inspect your work before asking for your pay.

Bonus idea: House painter's helper

Keep your eyes open for neighbors who are painting their house. Painters always need help. You may earn some cash, but more important, you'll improve your painting skills.

START-UP #41: CURB PAINTING

People in your neighborhood like to have their house number painted on the curb. It makes it easier for fire, police, or ambulance calls to be answered. It also helps friends and pizza delivery persons find the right house.

Most kids who start a curb-painting service charge $2 to $4 per job. It takes about 10 minutes to paint a house number on a curb. If you do three jobs an hour for $3 each, you've earned $9 a hour. It's not unusual for a curb-painting service to bring in $25 to $50 per day.

How to get started:

Read carefully to be sure you understand all the directions outlined below. Then practice painting your own house number on cardboard boxes. When you can make the numbers neat and readable, you'll be ready to go out and earn money.

Choose a street near your house with no numbers on the curbs. Go door-to-door explaining the benefits of your service. Once you get your first customer and others see how nice it looks, you will soon have many customers.

Supplies you'll need: Three sets of 3-inch stencils from an office supply store, a stiff brush, one can of black spray paint, one can of white spray paint, and half-sheet of poster board. You'll also need one or two plastic spines from those clear report covers you use in school.

Doing the job:

1. Cut a rectangle about 5 inches high and 15 inches wide in the center of the half-sheet of poster board to make a pattern for the background spray.

2. Before painting, brush any loose dirt off the curb with a stiff brush. Using your poster board pattern, spray the background rectangle white.

3. While the background paint drys a little, insert the correct house numbers in the plastic report cover spine.

4. Center the numbers over the background and tape them down. Spray the numbers black. Carefully lift the stencils. If everything looks good, collect your pay, and move on to the next customer.

5. If you ever make a mistake on a house number, paint over it completely with black paint. Let it dry. Then paint the correct number in white.

House numbers painted on curbs will usually last for 6 months or longer. When the numbers start getting hard to read, it will be time to go back through the neighborhood and sell your customers a touch-up or complete redo.

START-UP #42: THE MAILBOX DOCTOR

A mailbox is something homeowners use almost every day. Yet mailboxes in general are sadly neglected.

Take a walk or bike ride through your neighborhood and inspect mailboxes. You will find a few mailboxes that look like the owners really care. But many are badly in need of painting and few are adequately labeled.

Make it your business to solve mailbox problems. As The Mailbox Doctor, you can provide these services:

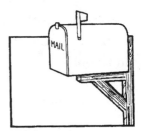

1. Clean dirty plastic mailboxes
2. Sand and paint old metal mailboxes
3. Personalize mailboxes with interesting designs
4. Decorate mailboxes for special holidays
5. Paint mailbox posts or stands
6. Label mailboxes with house numbers

How to get started:

Make some artistic flyers advertising yourself as The Mailbox Doctor. List typical services and fees.

Ask a few neighbors if you can do their mailbox free for practice. Take before-and-after photos of the mailboxes you "doctor."

Arrange the pictures in a photo album. Then start visiting homes with "sick" mailboxes and handing out your "prescriptions for good health."

·12·

HOW TO MAKE A PROFIT IN RETAIL SALES

WHEN IT COMES TO SELLING, NO ONE IS AS GOOD AT IT AS YOUNG PEOPLE. WHY? Because they practice all the time.

Have you ever convinced someone to watch your favorite TV show? Give you a ride? Let you stay out longer? Or loan you money? Each time you persuade another person to do something your way, you are selling.

In this chapter, you will have many opportunities to use your skills in sales. The 10 business start-ups described in the pages to follow are all based on selling a product that you either make or purchase from someone else.

Why a sales business is a great opportunity for young people:

1. Selling can be done by anyone. There's no age limit.
2. It's not physically demanding.
3. You can sell almost anywhere and any time.
4. There's no waiting or looking for jobs, because you're self-employed.
5. If you sell a product that gets used up quickly (it's consumable) and has to be replaced often (there's high demand), you have a source of unlimited income.
6. Once customers buy one product from you, they are likely to buy again and again if you keep providing good quality.

Difficulties to overcome in sales:

1. It's not always easy to find wholesale sources to get products or raw materials.

2. It takes more money for a start-up because you have to buy or manufacture the products you sell.

3. Products have to be stored somewhere until you sell them.

4. Some young people avoid selling things because they are afraid customers will say No.

WHAT TO DO WHEN THE CUSTOMER SAYS NO

No doesn't always mean "forever No." Sometimes it means the customer just isn't convinced yet. Study the following list of reasons people say No and how you might respond.

Why people say No:	What you can do:
1. They don't understand.	1. Tell them more about it.
2. They aren't sure they will like your product.	2. Show how it works; let them try it out.
3. They are afraid to spend the money.	3. Tell them about your other happy customers.
4. They don't have time right now.	4. Ask if you can come back another time.
5. They don't have the money right now.	5. Ask when is a better time.
6. They have already hired someone else.	6. Ask them to call if they need you later.
7. They truly don't need it.	7. Ask if they know someone who does.

There are two important rules to follow if you want to be successful in sales:

1. Represent only top-quality products that you have tried yourself and believe in. When you are convinced the product will improve the customer's quality of life, talking about your product is easy.

2. Determine who are your target customers—those most likely to need and want your product—and ask them first. Don't worry about the ones who say No. Just give good service to the ones who say Yes.

HOW TO MAKE MORE PROFIT IN SALES

Selling a product directly to the consumer is known as *retail sales*. The secret to making good money in a retail sales business is to buy your products at the lowest price possible. That means buying the product from a wholesaler or buying the raw materials and manufacturing the product for less. Then, when you sell the product to customers, you make an adequate profit to support and grow your business. Your goal should be to make at least 40% to 50% profit on every sale.

When Linh Huynh of San Francisco, California, was in eleventh grade, she signed up for a course on entrepreneurship offered at a local community center by the National Foundation for Teaching Entrepreneurship (NFTE). Valentine's Day was only a few weeks away, and Linh wanted to start a business selling gift boxes filled with assorted candies. She named her business Sensational Sweets Unlimited.

Then Linh ran into some problems. When she called candy wholesalers, she discovered they did not sell only 2 or 3 pounds of candy at a time. Their minimum order was a 100-pound bag, which cost at least $200. Linh didn't even have enough money to buy one bag of candy.

Since a candy business wasn't feasible, Linh began to look for other products she could buy wholesale and sell retail at a reasonable profit. An aunt helped her find a wholesaler that had pretty choker necklaces and pendants. When Linh showed samples of the jewelry to friends at school, they immediately wanted to buy them. Linh was confident it was time to launch her business.

Linh wrote a business plan and received a $50 grant from NFTE to purchase beginning inventory. Adding birthday money she had saved, Linh invested about $200 in her start-up. In addition to the necklaces, she also bought a variety of hair accessories, scented stationery, and stuffed animals.

Since she couldn't carry all these products around with her at school, Linh decided to create a gift catalog. She had been taking a workshop on photography, so she borrowed a camera and took pictures of all her products. Then Linh mounted the photos in a binder, wrote descriptions of the products, created order forms, and began to show her catalog to friends at school. Now when class is boring, friends often ask to see the catalog, and sales are going very well.

HOW TO GET STARTED

Looking back over her own start-up experience, Linh advises young entrepreneurs who want to start a retail business to "plan everything before you begin so there won't be any surprises like I had." These are some of her other suggestions for success:

1. Do your market research. Look for merchandise your customers want and need at a price they can afford.

2. Search for suppliers. You have to be able to buy wholesale in order to keep your prices competitive.

3. Plan your marketing strategies (Linh made a catalog).

4. Sell, sell, sell. Linh says, "When everything is going slow and you make a sale, you feel like you won the lottery."

5. Don't be pushy. When you push customers, they automatically resist. Be subtle, but friendly.

6. Stay close to your customers. Know what they need or want next, and find a way to get it for them.

START-UP #43: GIFT BASKETS

If you like to shop and enjoy being creative, the gift basket business is perfect for you. Your job will be to create and sell unusual baskets full of gift items centered around a theme. The theme should fit the special interests of the receiver.

Here are some examples of baskets you might create:

Holiday baskets centered around holiday themes

Souvenir baskets for out-of-state visitors

Birthday baskets, welcome baskets, or hostess baskets

Tea baskets full of gourmet teas and fresh muffins

Baby baskets for new mothers

Golf baskets or football baskets for sports lovers

Chocolate-filled baskets for chocolate-aholics

The variations and themes possible for gift baskets are endless. You will only be limited by your imagination and your resourcefulness in finding wholesale suppliers.

How to get started:

1. Choose one or two themes and make sample baskets. Take the baskets with you when you go out to sell.

2. Be sure to keep track of your cost of goods on every basket. Your retail price should be twice the cost of goods. Gift baskets can retail as high as $250, but you will do best staying in the $20 to $50 range in the beginning.

3. Charge extra for custom baskets because you will need extra time to shop. Ask customers how much they want to spend. Then explain what you can do for that price, and request a 50% deposit on the order.

The gift basket business is considered by many experts to be one of the hottest opportunities today. You will find competition in the market, but smart marketing will allow you to gain the advantage.

Ways to gain the competitive advantage:

1. *Lower overhead:* If your competitor operates a gift shop, she has to pay rent, utilities, and employees. You can operate from your home. Pass this savings along to your customers and sell your baskets for less.

2. *Location:* Remind your neighbors they don't have to drive all the way to the mall to buy a gift basket. They can shop from you anytime, even when the mall is closed. You can also provide free delivery.

3. *Quality:* You can offer freshly baked cookies or homemade muffins delivered in a gift basket on your customer's birthday. Your competitor has to buy cookies or muffins from a local bakery during normal business hours. Her cookies and muffins cost more and can't be as fresh as the ones you baked this morning and delivered.

START-UP #44: GIFT SERVICE

Busy people often have trouble remembering holidays, birthdays, and anniversaries. If they manage to remember the date, they don't have time to shop. You can help them solve this problem by operating a gift service.

Here's how it works:

1. Your most likely client will be a man or woman who owns a business, is a manager in a large company, or who runs a professional practice (doctor, lawyer, etc.). Market your services to them with flyers and personal visits to show your gift selections.

2. Offer your clients a selection of several attractive gift items you can wrap and deliver to their office the day before the important occasion. Good selections are baskets of fragrant potpourri, decorated cakes, flowers, plants, skin care products, inspirational books, jewelry, or stationery.

3. If you have friends who sell gift items, they may be willing to share the profits if you sell their products to your customers. This is a great way to increase the number of gift items you can provide without increasing your cash investment.

4. When customers sign up for your service, they pay a monthly fee for the reminders, plus the cost of the gifts. Get a list of the dates you are to remind the customer of. Then call the customer a week before the date and take the gift order. Tell customers the price over the phone, so they can leave payment at the office if you happen to deliver while they are out.

START-UP #45: FADS AND COLLECTIBLES

If it's the latest, the newest, the most popular, what's in, or cool—people spend money on it. Fads can make you money. Watch for good buys on things everyone wants or collects. Then buy extras and sell to friends at school or in your neighborhood.

Aron Schor, age 15, of Katonah, New York, has been collecting baseball cards for about 8 years and comic books for 2 or 3 years. He and his best friend, Alexxai Kravitz, recently started a mail order company to sell extra items from their personal collections. They call the business Dark Age Comics.

Aron and Alexxai used their computer to make an eight-page catalog of all the cards and comics they have for sale. Then they placed an ad in a local paper that most hobbyists read *(Comic Buyer's Guide)*. The ad costs $22 a month, but the first week they got 12 to 15 responses. They make copies of their catalog at the copy shop and send them out to inquirers. They also carry catalogs to school and give them away to friends who collect.

Aron says he isn't doing this to get rich, rather it's fun to meet and talk to other collectors. His advice for other young entrepreneurs is, "Don't take it too seriously. Do it just for the fun." And of course, you can always use the money you make to buy more stuff for your collection.

Suggestions for success:

No one can ever say what the next fad or collectible craze will be. If you view a collection as a long-term investment, you need to specialize in something very few people are now collecting. The ideal situation is to be one of very few people who own a collection like yours. Then the value of the collection remains very high.

If you view a fad or craze as a short-term opportunity to make money, your goal is to jump into the current fad and make money buying and selling now. Have fun with it. Then get out, before the fad ends or the prices go down.

START-UP #46: SCHOOL SPIRIT ITEMS

One of the fun things about going back to school in the fall is the beginning of football season. It's time to wear school colors, yell your lungs out, and get into the school spirit.

When football or basketball fever is high, students will buy anything with school colors or the team name: sweatshirts, book covers, hats, mugs, insulated drink holders, pens, tote bags, stadium cushions, hair ribbons, socks, calendars, towels, and more.

How to get started:

1. Start out with a school spirit item that you can make at home with low-cost supplies. Craft stores are a good place to get ideas. Make start-up money with this project.

1 Fast Cash for Kids

2. Then look under "advertising specialties" in your phone book. These businesses can supply almost any school spirit item you want. Ask them to send you a catalog.

3. Take a few samples of your product to school and start taking orders. By taking advance orders, you won't need very much start-up money. Sports fans in the community will want your products, also.

4. Wear or use your school spirit product everywhere you go. Get your friends to do the same. (At school you're with potential customers all day long, 5 days a week. But remember to stay within school rules about selling things.)

5. As your school spirit business catches on, watch for new trends and add new products to your line.

Bonus idea: Personalized items

A business that goes very well with the school spirit business is selling personalized items. You can put your customer's name on just about anything: belts, key chains, book bags, any article of clothing, Christmas ornaments, note cards, etc. You can sell these items all year long, not only at school but also throughout your neighborhood.

START-UP #47: BUMPER STICKERS

Bumper stickers are the sign boards of today's roadways. If you want to promote a cause, support a team, elect a candidate, or make people laugh, you can do it with a bumper sticker.

If you are interested in getting into this fun and profitable business, your first step will be to create a bumper sticker design that sells. Keep in mind that people read bumper stickers because they are entertaining. They buy bumper stickers because they identify with the message.

Success story: Kids for peace

Tommy Tighe, age 12, of Fountain Valley, California, started his bumper sticker business when he was 5 years old. Although he was only in kindergarten, Tommy was very aware of all the war and violence in the world. He couldn't understand why so many people wanted to fight and hurt others. One day Tommy decided it was his job to do something to promote world peace. He went into his bedroom and designed a simple bumper sticker that said, "Peace Please! Do It for Us Kids." That was the beginning of Kids for Peace.

After Tommy designed the bumper sticker, his next job was to find a way to get it printed. His parents helped him call printers to get quotes. Then Tommy had to find a way to raise enough money for the first printing of the bumper stickers.

While Tommy was working on this problem, he and his parents heard Mark Victor Hansen, a well-known author, speak at their church. The family met Mark Hansen afterwards. Hearing of Tommy's plan to sell bumper stickers to promote world peace, Mr. Hanson advised Tommy to write a business plan and apply for a grant from The Children's Free Enterprise Fund. Tommy received exactly enough money from the grant to pay for his first printing of 1,000 bumper stickers.

The next step in Tommy's plan was to launch a letter-writing campaign by children asking world leaders to find peaceful solutions to problems rather than start wars. When the newspapers found out about Tommy's mission, stories ran across the United States. Tommy also appeared as a guest on numerous television talk shows. The mail poured in, and Tommy spent hours every day after school filling orders for bumper stickers and writing personal thank-you letters to every customer.

Tommy proved that one kid who makes up his mind to do something about a cause can make a difference. When the Berlin Wall came down, Joan Rivers had Tommy on her show and presented him with a piece of the wall. Tommy had sent letters and bumper stickers to Russian leaders, pleading for peace.

Today, Tommy is considering other products such as T-shirts and book bags to add to his Kids for Peace business. He gets letters from school groups as far away as Singapore who want to sell the peace bumper stickers for fund-raisers. Tommy offers a wholesale discount when groups order 100 or more bumper stickers. The retail price is $3. If you want to sell Tommy's peace bumper stickers, write to him at 17283 Ward Street, Fountain Valley, CA 92708.

START-UP #48: SPECIAL PETS

If you love animals you may enjoy raising pets to sell. There are many animals you may chose to raise: birds, tropical fish, gerbils, rabbits, pure-bred cats and dogs, or even lizards. It's best to start with animals you know and enjoy already.

Where to get more information:

Pet stores will be glad to answer questions and help you get started. They may wish to sell the animals you raise. Also check with veterinarians for free booklets and information on the care of animals.

Local 4-H, FHA, and FFA clubs are very good places to meet other young people interested in animals. Most high schools offer courses through the vocational technology department that may be helpful.

Success story: Bays Bunny Barn

Emily Bays, a tenth-grader who lives in Alva, Oklahoma, has been raising rabbits since she was in fourth grade. She started raising them because they were so cute, not to earn money.

When Emily was in seventh grade, her parents built a 14-foot by 16-foot rabbit barn (rabbitry) so she could raise show rabbits. The new rabbitry is air conditioned, heated, and has an automatic watering system.

Emily says it takes time to learn how to raise quality show animals. She started attending more shows and learning more about the mini-lops as a breed. By the next year, she had won several ribbons. That was when Emily decided to have business cards printed advertising her business, Bays Bunny Barn.

Last year and this year, Emily's rabbits have won the mini-lop Best of Breed at the national convention of the American Rabbit Breeders Association. She had to beat 400 other entries to win that title.

Now that Emily is known as a national champion, she is starting to sell more rabbits. Other breeders want to buy from her to improve their litters. The most she has ever sold a single rabbit for is $150. She sold several at the most recent national show for $60 to $100.

Currently Emily has three litters of babies in the rabbitry. It takes about 10 minutes a day to care for the rabbits. On most weekends she spends 2 hours cleaning the barn and disinfecting cages.

If you want to raise mini-lops:

Emily Bays is president of the Mini-Lop Club of Oklahoma. Youths who want to raise mini-lops can write an essay about why they want to raise rabbits and send it to the Mini-Lop Club. If you qualify, you will receive three free rabbits (two does and one buck). You will be instructed on how to care for the rabbits. In return, you must agree to give someone else three rabbits at the end of 1 1/2 years. Get the forms by writing to Emily Bays, Mini-Lop Club of Oklahoma, 2015 Canyon Road, Alva, OK 73717.

START-UP #49: PERSONAL CARE ITEMS

Research shows that young teenage girls spend millions of dollars every year on cosmetics and skin care products. You go to school almost every day with girls that age. If they are going to spend all that money on skin care, nail care, hair products, and cosmetics, why not let them buy from you?

Thirteen-year-old Tamara Peschon of Webster, Texas, started helping a friend sell Avon products when she was 12. Tamara was getting so much business, she decided to work for herself. Since Tamara is under 18, her mother signed up as the Avon representative, but Tamara does the selling. Her mom only writes the checks when Tamara orders supplies.

Tamara enjoys selling the Avon products because the company brings out a new sales booklet every 2 weeks. All Tamara has to do is distribute 10 to 20 of the books to neighbors and teachers at school. Then she goes back in a few days when most of the customers have decided what they want to order. Because Avon runs new sales in each book, many women order every time a new book comes out.

Expenses for Tamara's Avon business include the cost of the books, samples, and advertising brochures. But Tamara is pleased because she makes about 20% to 35% on every sale. The company has an excellent reputation for quality and does a great deal of advertising to support the sales representatives.

Becoming a representative for a company like Avon, Mary Kay Cosmetics, or Amway is one of the easiest ways to get into the business of selling personal care items. There is usually a minimum purchase required, however, and none of the companies will work with you directly if you are under 18. That means you will have to team up with an older friend or relative if you want to represent these product lines. However, these companies do have excellent training programs, and you will learn a great deal about marketing, sales, and business organization.

START-UP #50: LOCKER IN A BAG

What happens when teachers say, "Don't forget?" Kids do forget (or run out) of all kinds of school supplies: folders, notebooks, map pencils, markers, 3 × 5 cards, rulers, graph paper, typing paper, and many other items. Solve this problem by turning your backpack into a business called Locker in a Bag, a mobile school supply store.

Buy extra school supplies when they are on sale, or buy large packages of favorite items from office supply warehouses. Then divide the packages and resell the supplies when classmates need things for school. Most kids won't even mind if they have to pay a little more for the supplies. They know they are also getting free delivery. You may even save some kids from getting a bad grade because they don't have proper supplies.

START-UP #51: FAVORITE BOOKS

Almost anyone can start a business selling books. If you read a book that you really like, look on the title page to find the publisher's name. Then ask the reference person at the public library to help you find the publisher's address and phone number.

Call or write the publisher a letter asking about the wholesale price on the book. Smaller publishing houses are almost always willing to work with someone who wants to sell books. You can expect a 40% discount on your purchases. Some publishers will require you to purchase as many as 50 books to get this discount. Some give the discount to any bookseller, with no minimum purchase required.

How to have fun with a book business:

Sell a group of titles about your favorite hobby. Since you already love the subject, you won't have any problem talking to customers. For example, you might sell five of the best titles on collecting baseball cards, training dogs, cake decorating, or making jewelry. Your target customers will be people who share your hobby.

Publishing and selling your own book:

David Kahl, Jr., of Fargo, North Dakota, published his own book when he was in fifth grade. He titled it *Better Letters*. The book comes in a three-ring binder with pockets and straps to hold pens, pencils, postcards, note paper, and other writing materials. It con-

tains 65 pages of instructions for kids on how to write all kinds of letters (thank-you letters, business letters, letters for special occasions, etc.) and lists of mailing addresses of professional sports teams, TV networks, tourist offices, and other interesting sources. David updates the mailing addresses every year.

Today David is in eighth grade, and *Better Letters* is sold in several local bookstores around Fargo. David is frequently asked to speak in schools throughout the state about his publishing business. He sells a great many of his books through word-of-mouth, trade shows, and his school appearances. His average annual book sales usually total $3,000 to $4,000. This year David is trying a new form of marketing—sponsoring a third-grade Little League team. The jerseys he furnishes the team say Better Letters.

David is now in the process of releasing two more books. The first is *Book of Fame,* which is a book parents can use to collect memories and record events of their child's first 12 years. The other new book is *Keys to Kid Care*, a book for day care workers to communicate with parents about their child's daily activities and progress. For mail order information about David's books, write Midland Instructional Creations, P.O. Box 5722, Fargo, ND 58105.

START-UP #52: BALLOONS

Margaux Nguyen is a student at the University of Houston College of Business Administration. This year she started a business called World of Balloons, which specializes in balloon bouquets and decorating with balloons for special events. Margaux also sells balloon bouquets attached to fruit baskets, sweetheart bouquets, cookie bouquets, candy bouquets, and balloons stuffed with flowers and toys.

Although Margaux invested over $4,000 to buy special machinery and start her company, she says a balloon business is possible for young entrepreneurs who have very little start-up capital.

How to get started:

1. Margaux advises starting with plain latex or mylar balloons filled with helium. She says balloon wholesalers are fairly easy to locate. The average price for a *gross* of balloons (144 balloons) is currently about $5.

2. Although a single balloon costs less than 4 cents, you will also have the expense of renting a helium tank and buying a preservative to make balloons last longer. Compare prices before you choose suppliers.

3. Margaux advises composing a price list of your products with single balloons selling for about 85 cents and bouquets in the $15 to $20 price range.

4. Use your creativity with ribbons, streamers, and small favors to make balloons more attractive. Bouquets can be attached to stuffed animals, boxes of candy, or any type of gift item.

5. Learn about decorating with balloons by observing other caterers and decorators, reading books, or contacting balloon manufacturers for special instructions.

6. Boost sales by teaming up with schools, clubs, and organizations to put on fund-raisers. For example, the junior class could raise money by selling balloon bouquets for Valentine's Day. Have them start taking orders several weeks in advance. You make the bouquets and split the profits with the class.

Growing your business

Margaux says she has always known she wanted to start her own business, even in high school. Like most young entrepreneurs, Margaux keeps expenses down by working from home. She has no employees, but sales are expanding rapidly, and she is writing a business plan for a full-service balloon, gift, and flower shop she hopes to open next year.

Margaux has been accepted into a special program at the University of Houston where she receives extensive training in entrepreneurship. She is sure she would never have had the courage to invest her savings to start World of Balloons if it hadn't been for the support of the University of Houston Center for Entrepreneurship & Innovation. She recommends that young entrepreneurs seek university-level training, so that they have a greater chance of success in business.

·13·

How to Make Money Selling Food

FOOD IS BIG BUSINESS. WHY? BECAUSE FOOD IS A BASIC NECESSITY OF LIFE. EVERYBODY eats! Everybody spends money on food. Everybody likes food. Everybody needs food. If you sell only a very tiny percentage of the food bought in your town every day, you can make a nice income as part of the food industry.

Advantages of a business selling food:

1. Food is a universal need. Everyone you meet is a potential customer. And you can sell to the same customers over and over, day after day.

2. Lots of busy people are willing to buy food rather than prepare it themselves. Today more people in our society eat out or buy prepared foods daily than ever before.

3. Anyone can learn to prepare good food. If you want a business in food preparation, you can find plenty of free information on how to do it.

4. The need for food will never end. As long as you provide a high-quality product at a reasonable price, you can stay in business as long as you want.

Disadvantages of a business selling food:

1. You have to really like food preparation, or you'll get tired of the business very quickly.

2. It is an absolute must that you adhere to strict health and sanitation standards in food handling. You will also need to check with local authorities to see if licenses or inspections are required.

3. Start-up costs could be high if you have to buy special cookware, bakeware, appliances, or equipment to keep foods at proper temperatures.

4. What you don't sell could spoil, so you will need to carefully plan your marketing strategies and storage facilities.

THE SECRET OF SUCCESS: MOBILITY

For young entrepreneurs, the key to being involved in the food industry is mobility. You will not invest large sums of money to open a restaurant, grocery store, or bakery. To compete in the food industry, you will do what most of these businesses cannot do. You will go to the customer. You will be a mobile lunch counter, a mobile snack shop, or a mobile ice cream stand that finds the customer wherever he is working or living. You will provide on-the-spot delivery, making it more convenient to do business with you than with the restaurant ten blocks away. You will gain the competitive advantage in a small niche market, and you will make money doing it.

START-UP #53: LUNCH MAKERS

People who carry lunches to work or school everyday get very tired of making sandwiches and trying to think of new ways to make lunch interesting. They need someone like you to specialize in creating healthy lunches to go.

What you need to get started:

1. Recipes or directions for making really big, hearty, healthy, munchy sandwiches that taste fantastic

2. Several additional items to go with sandwiches: fruit salad, apple cobbler, homemade granola, stuffed celery, popcorn balls, etc.

3. Start-up money to buy enough ingredients for the first day's lunches

4. Flyers or menus to advertise your lunches

Here's how it works:

1. Determine how much it costs to make each item on your menu and make flyers with a menu and price list.

2. Show your menus to friends, family, neighbors, or teachers and take orders for lunches 1 or 2 days in advance.

3. Buy the ingredients and make the lunches at night before you go to bed. (After you get into a routine, you may be able to get up early in the morning and make the lunches.)

4. Deliver the lunches in the morning before school, or take the lunches with you to school and deliver them. Collect your money and get the orders for the next day.

5. Study recipe books and magazines for new ideas. Change your lunches frequently so customers don't get bored. Always do something creative that makes your lunch better than the lunches they make for themselves at home.

START-UP #54: MOBILE SWEET SHOP

Turn your backpack into a mobile sweet shop, and you can sell all kinds of candy, fudge, brownies, cookies, or dessert bars to your friends all year long.

Suggestions for success:

1. First you need a recipe for a sweet treat that's really special. Frosted brownies or giant chocolate-chip cookies with huge chunks of chocolate and pecans are old standbys that always sell. If you're creative in the kitchen, invent a recipe for something people can't get anywhere else.

2. Figure out a safe way to wrap and protect your baked item or candy so it stays fresh.

3. If you don't want to bake, you can get into this business by purchasing big boxes of candy at warehouse stores and reselling it at competitive prices.

4. Sell your sweets during school lunch, before or after school, at ball games, club meetings, craft fairs, or anywhere people gather.

5. Offer to take special orders for parties or holidays.

START-UP #55: CHILDREN'S CAKES

Cake decorating is a skill that pays well and is in high demand. The best way to learn is to take a class, then spend some time practicing. After you feel fairly confident of your skills, you can start a business selling decorated cakes for children's birthdays or holiday parties. Children's cakes are easier to make and transport because they are usually flat cakes baked in shaped pans rather than layer cakes.

How to get started:

Study cake-decorating books and get ideas for at least five or six designs you will offer in the beginning. Make a sample of each cake and take color pictures. Mount the pictures in an album, with notes describing the cakes and your prices. Each time you create a new cake, remember to add its picture to your album.

You will need some start-up money to invest in baking pans, decorating tubes, tips, cake ingredients, and candles. And you will need to make some colorful flyers announcing your children's cakes for all occasions. Once you sell a few cakes, you will start getting customers by word-of-mouth.

START-UP #56: FOOD NOVELTIES AND GIFTS

For a creative person, inventing and selling food novelties is a wonderful business opportunity. The concept is to take a popular food product, package it in creative serving ware, give your creation an offbeat name, and sell it as a novelty gift item. For example, you might package animal crackers in a colorful plastic boat and call it Noah's Ark of Treats. Every kid will want at least one. And when the crackers are gone, there's a toy left to play with.

How to get started:

1. Spend some time brainstorming ideas for creative food novelties. Start with food that won't easily spoil, such as trail mix, snack mixes, candy, gourmet popcorn, spice mixes, or a bean soup mix.

2. Then add some unusual packaging ideas like sand pails, fish bowls, straw hats, miniature garbage cans, mugs, doggie bowls, tins, or canisters. Use your imagination to give the item you create a catchy name.

3. Then test the new product by asking friends and neighbors for their opinion. If it's well-received, go full-steam-ahead with the marketing of your idea.

Books to read:

Mrs. Witty's Monster Cookies by Helen Witty. A collection of award-winning recipes for making super-size cookies (Workman Publishing).

Baking Projects for Children by Fran Stephens. Easy-to-understand directions on how to make gingerbread houses, decorated cookies, and cookie bouquets (Murdoch Books).

START-UP #57: MOBILE LEMONADE STAND

Most people today aren't driving up and down the streets looking for lemonade stands. But every kid loves to sell lemonade. What can you do to attract customers?

If the customers won't come to you, go to them. Put your lemonade stand on a wagon and make it mobile. Take it to the park, across the street from the drive-in window at the bank, the local tennis courts, the golf course, or jogging tracks. Or ask permission to set up your stand at a neighbor's garage sale.

Other ways to update:

1. Plan your lemonade sale for the day of the week when your neighborhood is the busiest, usually a Saturday.

2. Attract attention with signs, balloons, streamers, or banners. Provide music or entertainment, if possible. Put on puppet shows, dress like a clown, or do gymnastics.

3. Update your lemonade recipe by adding special ingredients like club soda, chopped candied fruit, or a twist of lemon. You can also freeze your lemonade and sell it as popsicles or slush.

4. Offer additional choices such as iced tea, orange juice, or cold canned drinks. Offer brownies or homemade cookies for sale.

For more ideas about improving your lemonade stand, read *Start Your Own Lemonade Stand* by Steven Caney (Workman Publishing).

START-UP #58: HOME BAKERY

High-quality home-baked breads, cakes, and pies are always in great demand. If you enjoy baking and have access to a kitchen, this could be a very good business for you.

The current most popular bakery items are muffins, health breads, cheesecakes, carrot cakes, international specialties, or any low-fat and sugar-free dessert. Don't try to offer everything. The best way to start a successful home bakery is to specialize in one product and do it extremely well.

How to get started:

1. Choose one bakery item to begin your business. Best ideas are family recipes that have been developed and improved from generation to generation.

2. Test the recipe to be sure it consistently produces the quality of product you need to build a business. Test ideas for improvements, and figure the exact cost to prepare each recipe.

3. Determine who is your most likely market. Set your prices, and make flyers advertising your product. Start marketing to individuals you know first.

4. Consider making a deal with a local restaurant that you will supply with a certain number of cakes or gourmet muffins daily or weekly. Many restaurants buy from private bakeries because they want something distinctive and unusual.

5. Get permission to take baskets of your baked items to a nearby office building on Friday afternoons. Go from office to office delivering orders or selling freshly baked goods workers can take home for the weekend.

START-UP #59: FITNESS FOODS

People who are really concerned about fitness are very particular about the meals and snacks they eat. They often have difficulty finding something healthy to eat when they attend sports events, go shopping, travel, or visit public places. If you are tuned into fitness, you understand this market well. Fitness foods could be a very good business for you.

How to get started:

1. Look for a warehouse or wholesale outlet where you can get good prices on favorite fitness foods such as popcorn, trail mix, raisins, granola, whole-grain crackers, rice cakes, cheese spreads, health bars, boxed juices, and bottled water. Choose four or five products to sell.

2. Sell your fitness foods from your duffle bag, backpack, sports bag, or insulated bag at swim meets, tennis courts, sports tournaments, team practices, fun runs, along biking trails, or anywhere fitness enthusiasts gather.

3. Freeze juices the night before and use them to keep other foods cool. As they thaw, they make delightful slushlike treats.

4. Wear a T-shirt or jacket that identifies your business. Establish a regular schedule of when and where you sell, so that your customers can depend on you.

START-UP #60: HOT DRINKS

Start a business providing hot drinks for people working or playing out of doors in cold weather. The colder the weather, the better your business will be.

Make jugs of hot chocolate, hot cider, spiced tea, or gourmet coffee. Wrap the jugs in towels for extra insulation. Sell from a wagon, cart, table, or with a sign on top of your car. Serve drinks in styrofoam cups so they stay warm longer. Get additional business by offering several high-energy snack foods. People need extra calories in weather like this.

Remember, your customers won't come to you. You have to go to them—even in cold weather.

START-UP #61: TAILGATE ENTERPRISES

If you drive or have a friend who drives, consider turning your vehicle into a business asset. The tailgate or trunk of your car can become a snowcone shop, a donut shop, a hot dog stand, barbecue stand, fruit stand, or almost any other enterprise.

Suggestions for success:

You will have to plan carefully so that foods are kept at proper temperatures and handled safely. Prepackage everything as much as possible. Use one ice chest for hot foods and a second ice chest for cold foods. Carry water to wash hands, and wear disposable plastic gloves when handling food.

Put a sign on top of your car and sell foods in the parking lot at local sports events, Little League games, parades, camping or recreational areas, or before and after school. The general idea is to show up with food where people are hungry and thirsty. Be sure to ask permission or get permits if required.

START-UP #62: ICE CREAM VENDOR

When Ben Cohen and Jerry Greenfield first started Ben & Jerry's Ice Cream, they almost never went anywhere without a trunk full of ice cream on dry ice. Whenever they saw an office building or likely place where customers would gather, they would stop and start giving away samples. Ben & Jerry became known as two real guys who built a business that cares about its customers.

You can apply these concepts to start your own ice cream business. (If Ben & Jerry can, so can you.)

How to get started:

1. Do research to find good suppliers for ice cream bars and frozen confections. Like Ben & Jerry, insist on high quality that attracts the upscale customer.

2. Make a sign listing your products and prices.

3. Pack your ice cream in an ice chest with dry ice. (Always wear gloves to handle dry ice.) Then set the ice chest in a wagon or cart that you can pull behind your bike. Attach your sign where it's easy to see.

4. Ride up and down the streets in your neighborhood, stopping to tell friends and neighbors about your ice cream delivery service. Stimulate sales by giving out coupons for a special offer.

5. Start an ice cream club for kids. Give out membership cards they get signed each time they buy ice cream. When they've made six purchases, give them something free.

6. Go to parks, tennis courts, practice fields, or wherever you can find groups of people. After customers buy from you one or two times, they'll start watching for you. Try to go on the same route at about the same time every day.

START-UP #63: CATERING SERVICES

GET CREATIVE

Brad Boisvert, age 17, of Warwick, Rhode Island, owns and operates a catering business called The Perfect Edible Centerpiece. Although Brad has always been interested in cooking, he didn't start making edible centerpieces until he was 9.

That year, Brad attended an all-day food design demonstration presented by a group of culinary students at a mall. He was absolutely fascinated as he watched the students carve flowers and animals out of beets, onions, cabbages, squash, and colorful fruits. After watching the students all day, Brad went home and tried it himself. He hasn't stopped learning since.

At first Brad's centerpieces were just for friends and family members who saw his creations and requested them for holiday dinners. But by age 11, Brad had improved enough that his hobby had actually become a business. He had business cards printed and bought produce in bulk from restaurant suppliers and wholesalers. In fifth grade, he joined Junior Achievement Club, so he could learn more about operating a business.

Today Brad averages working in his business about 20 hours a week. He sells edible centerpieces for all occasions, as well as pastries, decorated cakes, and complete meals. He caters banquets, award dinners, receptions, weddings, baby showers, or any special event. Brad says his average catering job usually involves serving 150 people at a time. Most of his clients come from word-of-mouth referrals.

When Brad isn't preparing for an event, he spends his extra time updating the business records, tracking down new suppliers, comparing prices, and looking for ways to improve his skills. Brad is now president of his Junior Achievement chapter and state president of the VICA (Vocational Industrial Club of America) clubs in Rhode Island. He also works as a line cook and assistant chef at a local restaurant.

Everything Brad does is planned toward achieving his goal of becoming a certified master chef. After high school, it takes at least 12 years to attain this level. There are currently only 40 certified master chefs in the world.

If you are interested in learning the business of catering, Brad offers these suggestions for success:

1. Make sure you really love food and cooking before you start a catering business. If you enjoy what you do, it doesn't seem like work.

2. Don't let being young stop you from working toward your goal. If you really want to learn, you can find a way.

3. Join clubs and organizations that teach you about business. Brad suggests Junior Achievement and VICA.

4. Work for other caterers or restaurants so you can learn the business in a hands-on situation. One deli Brad worked for even let him put up signs advertising his catering services.

5. Invest in the best kitchen utensils and tools to do your job right. Brad always knows what is the next piece of equipment he needs to purchase.

6. Watch your expenses closely. Always know what the profit margin is on every job you quote.

7. Cooperate with your family, especially if you are using the family kitchen. Brad and his mother often plan family meals together and Brad cooks almost every night he's home. He also treats the family to his best catering services on holidays.

For information about Junior Achievement programs, write to the national headquarters at One Education Way, Colorado Springs, CO 80906 (719-540-8000).

·14·

How to Turn a Profit in Crafts

IF YOU ENJOY HANDCRAFTS AND HAVE THE ABILITY TO MAKE LARGE QUANTITIES OF one item in a small amount of time, a craft business is a good opportunity for you. In fact, craft businesses are a favorite money-making enterprise for young entrepreneurs.

Advantages of a craft business:

1. It's fun to get paid to participate in a hobby you already enjoy.

2. It's easy to create new products to sell because you have a talent for your craft.

3. You already have most of the tools, supplies, and training you need.

4. You're familiar with the average prices, favorite colors and styles, and type of customers who buy your product.

5. More information is easy to find. You know other crafters, craft stores, suppliers, and places to take classes.

Drawbacks of a craft business:

1. Prices on craft items are very competitive. It is often difficult to sell crafts for a high enough price to give you a decent hourly wage.

2. In a craft business, you often need to manufacture a high volume of your product in a short period of time. Even if you love the craft, repetition is boring.

3. If you have good ideas, other crafters will start copying your work. To stay ahead of your competitors, you must continue learning about your craft and keep introducing new products.

REQUIREMENTS FOR SUCCESS

A craft business requires creative talent as well as business know-how. As the owner of a craft business, you will have many jobs. You are the "chief creative officer" who invents the product. Then you are the worker who manufactures the product. After that, you are the marketing representative, the sales clerk, and the delivery person. And on top of everything, you're president of the company!

The key to success in crafts is choosing products that are cost effective. It is not cost effective to make needlepoint pillows that take 40 hours of labor to create but only sell for $25. You'll be making less than 60 cents an hour.

The ideal craft item for mass production sells for a high enough price to pay you at least minimum wage. A good example is handmade jewelry. Jewelry makers interviewed for this chapter report that it takes about 30 minutes to make a necklace. Investment for materials may be as high as $6, but the necklace sells for $12 or more. On this project you would make at least $6 an hour.

FAVORITE MARKETING METHODS

Many of your creations will be sold directly to friends, neighbors, and relatives who happen to see what you're doing and want to make a purchase. However, these sales will not be enough to sustain a long-term business. You must have a system of marketing that puts you in contact with new customers regularly.

The four best ways to market craft products:

1. *Door-to-door sales:* Use a briefcase or portfolio to carry samples of your products. Visit residences as well as offices, particularly around holiday gift-buying seasons.
2. *Consignment agreements:* Resale shops, boutiques, and small privately owned stores often like to carry items made by local crafts people. Compare commissions before you choose your locations.
3. *Craft shows:* Watch local papers for advance notices of craft shows and fairs. Most shows charge booth rental fees. Stick with shows that cost about $25 to participate.

4. *Flea markets:* The best thing about flea markets is that they are usually open year round. Tables or booths are fairly inexpensive, and a flea market is the easiest way for young entrepreneurs to have a permanent retail location. If you are under 18, a parent may have to cosign your contract.

SALES TECHNIQUES

J'Morgan Washington, age 14, of Richmond, Virginia, loves selling things. It doesn't matter what the product is. She's sold everything from keychains to candy. Sometimes she enters sales contests just because she enjoys competing to see who can sell the most.

J'Morgan learned a lot of her sales techniques by working in her father's chicken restaurant when she was younger. She also worked in a flea market with her friend's grandmother. J'Morgan is currently in the process of opening a silk-screened T-shirt business and thinking about opening her own booth in a flea market.

These are some of J'Morgan's suggestions for selling things in a flea market or craft show:

1. Pay attention to every customer. Greet everyone and treat them all equally.

2. Be cheerful and confident of yourself. People like to buy from you when you are fun to be around.

3. Be willing to make a deal as long as it's reasonable. Give your customers a bargain.

4. When customers keep wanting you to go lower and lower on your price, say No.

J'Morgan advises caution when a customer wants to bargain or haggle over prices. Remember that each time you go down on the price, you give away a little more of your profit. J'Morgan sets a "bottom line" that she will not pass. Then she tells the customer, "That's my bottom line. I have to make something for my work, or I can't stay in business." Most people understand and respect her statement.

START-UP #64: HANDMADE JEWELRY

Making and selling handmade jewelry is one of the favorite youth entrepreneurship business projects today. Young people like it because they get to be creative and because they can usually make a finished product in less than 30 minutes.

Emily Burdick, age 11, who lives in Houston, Texas, has a business she calls Emilina's Original Jewelry Designs. Her first products were beaded eyeglass chains that her aunt taught her how to make. When Emily discovered she could invest $4 to $6 in materials, make a chain in 20 minutes, and sell it for $10 to $15, she decided to create additional products. Today Emily sells a line of handmade stickpins and earrings that take about 5 minutes each to make and sell for $5 to $10. She also sells children's bracelets and a product she calls a "body cross," which is a beaded belt that crisscrosses the chest and wraps the waist.

According to Emily, most jewelry is easy to make. She says, "Most things that look complicated are really easy once you find out how it's done." She found that craft stores were very helpful. She gets her ideas for designs by watching what people wear, attending craft shows, and studying the craft store displays.

Michelle Weil, age 10, in Highland Park, Illinois, learned how to make jewelry by following directions in kits she bought at craft stores. After understanding the basics, Michelle started creating her own designs for beaded rings, bracelets, and necklaces. Her business is called Michelle's Majestic Boutique.

Both Emily and Michelle sell most of their jewelry by word-of-mouth to friends and family members. They have also done very well selling from tables in craft fairs and art fairs. Here are some of their tips for success in fairs:

1. Several months before the show, decide how much jewelry you need, and set a work schedule to get it all done.

2. Make an attractive sign that is easy to read. Plan a way to hang it, or bring a stand for the sign. Michelle found that signs attached to the front of the table cannot be seen, and customers often accidentally knock them down.

3. Both girls say an attractive, well-planned booth is very important. They recommend using colorful tablecloths to make the jewelry stand out.

4. Emily suggests using folding screens as a backdrop and as a place to hang necklaces. She puts small items like bracelets in baskets.

5. Michelle emphasizes that your table should never be allowed to get messy or jumbled. She uses wooden mug holders and plastic towel racks to hang jewelry.

START-UP #65: KEY CHAIN BUSINESS

Katie Conelly, age 16, of St. Paul, Minnesota, started her key chain business with guidance from the National Foundation for Teaching Entrepreneurship (NFTE). Under the business name K-T's Keychains, Katie manufactures and sells southwestern style key chains made with metal conchos and multicolored beads on leather strings.

Like jewelry, key chains can be made in large quantities in a small amount of time. Katie invests about $2.50 in supplies and spends about 10 minutes to produce each key chain she sells for $5.

Her advice for other young entrepreneurs who want to start this business is to "have faith in your product and act with confidence." She sold 100 keychains during the first 2 weeks she was in business.

Marketing methods:

Katie believes word-of-mouth is the best advertising, but she also hands out flyers and puts some of her key chains on consignment at a local boutique. Anytime she can sell from a table at the shopping center or at a public event, Katie takes the opportunity.

Katie's most effective marketing strategy is making key chains in school colors, team colors, and ethnic colors. Active in volleyball, softball, and hockey, Katie sells a lot of key chains to her teammates. Around Christmas, she uses the advertising slogan "Big enough to find in your purse, but small enough to put in a stocking." In 1994, Katie was chosen to receive one of NFTE's Young Entrepreneur of the Year awards.

START-UP #66: CANDLE CRAFTS

Candles are appropriate for all occasions. They make wonderful decorations for the home, and they make great gifts any time of the year. If you are interested in a candle-making business, you can get started by trying this idea for ice cube candles.

How to make ice cube candles:

1. Collect old candles or buy wax by the block. Bend the rim of an empty coffee can to form a spout. Put wax in the coffee can. Place on a rack in a pot of water. Melt wax over low heat.

2. Tint the wax with old crayons. Or you can buy dyes and scents from a craft store.

3. Use a $1/2$-half gallon or 1-quart milk carton for a mold. Prepare the wick by tying a heavy washer or fishing weight to one end. Suspend it over the center of your mold with a pencil.

4. For an interesting and unusual candle, fill the mold with ice cubes. Then carefully pour hot wax into the mold without disturbing the wick.

5. Allow the candle to cool overnight. Tear the paper carton away from the candle and drain the water.

6. Decorate with ribbon, Christmas greenery, silk flowers, glitter, or whipped wax. Sell to friends and neighbors or take special orders.

Craft stores have books on how to make many kinds of candles. Almost anything can be used as a mold: frozen-juice containers, muffin tins, or even egg shells. Some candles such as dipped candles, roll-up candles, and free-form candles (made by pouring wax in cold water and molding it with your fingers) don't need molds. The candle business is an opportunity to get paid for using your creativity and imagination.

START-UP #67: SHELL CRAFTS

Shells of differing sizes, shapes, and colors are fun to work with. They can be glued together to look like funny animals, space creatures, flowers, or even people. Shells can be used to make jewelry or to decorate mirrors, picture frames, and baskets. You can glue them on boxes, arrange them in pictures, or mount them in frames. There is almost no limit to what you can create with sea shells.

If you are a very artistic person, you will enjoy painting scenes on large sand dollars. These paintings can be created very quickly, and they can make a sand dollar worth four to five times it's wholesale price.

How to get started in a shell craft business:

1. If you live near the coast, you may be able pick up shells for free right off the beaches. Otherwise, to make a profit in this business, you will need a good wholesale supplier.

2. Start your business by offering only two or three shell creations. Concentrate on learning to market these effectively before you bring out more new products.

3. Make samples of several shell creations, and show them to people in your neighborhood. Take an informal survey to find out which items your target customers like best.

4. Look for boutiques and gift shops that will carry your shell crafts on consignment.

START-UP #68: STUFFED TOYS AND PUPPETS

Soft, cuddly stuffed animals, toys, dolls, and puppets never go out of style. Use your creativity to invent stuffed toys and puppet characters people can't buy anywhere else. Market your products at craft fairs, flea markets, and consignment shops. Holidays will be excellent for your business.

How to get started:

1. Visit toy stores and gift shops for ideas. Specialize in something you love: clowns, teddy bears, funny monsters, school mascots, or rag dolls.

2. To learn how to make puppets from almost anything, read the book *The Muppets Make Puppets* by Cheryl Henson (Workman Publishing, 1994).

3. Gather materials you can work with. Friends and relatives may save scraps or give you leftover craft materials if they know what you're doing. Show them your plans and ask for their input.

4. A good marketing strategy is to give your toys or puppets names. Then write a story with your toy or puppet as the character and include a copy with each purchase.

START-UP #69: BUTTONS AND BADGES

Joseph Pride, age 13, and Theodore Pride, age 15, are brothers in Fenton, Missouri, who started a badge business almost 4 years ago. Their parents, Bill and Mary Pride, write and publish books on home schooling. This gives Joseph and Theodore an ideal niche market for selling badges with favorite home school slogans. Most of the badges and magnets they make are sold at home school conventions or through their parents' home school catalog.

Joseph and Theodore advise anyone starting this business to invest in a top-quality button press. They have used several machines themselves but prefer the Badge-A-Matic 1 for reliability, speed, and cost effectiveness. (For information on this machine, write to: Badge-A-Minit, 348 North 30th Road., LaSalle, IL 61301.)

Average profit on each badge, according to Joseph and Theodore, is about $1. It takes less than 3 minutes to make a button, badge, or magnet. However, it does take some time and imagination to create attractive, eye-catching designs that appeal to a wide variety of buyers.

Buttons, badges, and magnets are great items to personalize with your customer's name, favorite team, business name, or favorite saying. Offer to work with clubs and organizations that need badges or buttons for special events.

START-UP #70: WREATHS

Today wreaths are used to decorate the home year round, not just during holidays. Grapevine wreaths, for example, are very popular for all-occasion decorating. However, wreaths made from dried flowers, wheat, pinecones, sweetgum balls, nuts, colorful fall leaves, and even sea shells are also in great demand. The beauty of this business is that nature provides most of the materials absolutely free. And you can find instructions for making the wreaths free at your public library.

How to make a grapevine wreath:

In many parts of the country, wild grapevines are plentiful. Gather grapevines (or Clematis vines) when they are green and cut them in 6- to 7-foot lengths. Strip off the leaves, but leave the curly tendrils. Bend one vine into an 18-inch circle to form the base. Wind it around, going over and under several times, so it stays together. Then add another vine, weaving it through the first vine. Gradually add about five to six more vines, until you have a nice, firm wreath. Lay the wreath flat to dry in a warm place. Decorate with a plaid ribbon and other findings you've collected from nature's "craft store."

START-UP #71: RECYCLING THROW-AWAYS

Keeya Branson of Philadelphia, Pennsylvania, was a senior in high school when she started a business called NEO Enterprises. Workmen had left behind a lot of copper wire and telephone wire in a classroom where Keeya was taking a course sponsored by the National Foundation for Teaching Entrepreneurship (NFTE). One day in class, Keeya got an idea to make a bracelet out of the free wire. She took the wire bracelet home and added some metal and wooden beads. The next day, everyone at school wanted to know where she got the unusual jewelry.

Soon Keeya was selling $3 bracelets and $5 earrings as fast as she could make them. Keeya eventually developed a whole line of products made from free wire, including necklaces, bracelets, earrings, anklets, and rings. One of her best marketing techniques was to make each earring different, so there were no matched pairs. Customers liked the idea of mixing and matching, and happily paid $5 per earring for Keeya's creations.

NEO Enterprises also provided Keeya a nice income during her first year of college. Today she is 23, has a degree in philosophy, and owns a public relations agency in Philadelphia called Wide Awake Publicity. In 1994, she was selected Honorable Entrepreneur of the Year by NFTE.

Suggestions for success:

If making things from throw-away materials sounds like a good business idea to you, start looking around your home and community to see what you can find. It is very likely you will discover sources of scrap wood, wire, tile, buckets, paper, cardboard, plastics, and many other items. It will take imagination and research to invent a marketable product, but the result could be a very profitable business.

START-UP #72: GREETING CARDS AND STATIONERY

Kelly Hayden and Kylie Dohman, both age 13, are best friends and co-owners of a business called KK Kards in Littleton, Colorado. They sell bookmarks, stationery, and custom-designed greeting cards for all occasions.

Kelly and Kylie got started making cards for fun when a neighbor gave Kelly some leftover stickers. The first card they sold was a thank-you card to Kelly's younger brother, Matt. After seeing their work, Kelly's mom gave the girls some supplies she had left from a rubber stamp business. Then Kelly and Kylie made an office in the basement and decided to go into business.

How to get started:

1. Kelly and Kylie learned a lot about their craft from Kelly's mom and aunt and by watching videos. Being an apprentice is Kylie's favorite way of learning.

2. They advise anyone starting this business to invest in an embossing gun (sort of like a hair dryer) that blows hot air. Expect to pay about $30 for this tool. Kelly and Kylie use the gun on most of their designs.

3. You will use a lot of paper and cardstock in this business, so you need a good supplier. Kelly and Kylie buy paper by the pound at Paperware.

4. Open a savings account for your business. KK Kards has an account at Young Americans Bank, where Kelly and Kylie both serve on the Youth Advisory Board. The bank also hosts monthly meetings of the YES Club, which helps Kelly and Kylie meet other young entrepreneurs, hear experienced guest speakers, and learn more about running a business.

5. Much of your work will be sold by word-of-mouth. However, Kelly and Kylie found it helpful to make a portfolio of their designs. When they showed the portfolio to Linda Sanders, President of Young Americans Bank, they got an order for 100 Christmas cards.

6. Kylie says that when you get big orders, you have to discipline yourself to work even when you don't feel like it. But once you get started, you get more in the mood.

7. Price your work reasonably so that customers get a bargain if they buy from you rather than from a store. Most of Kelly and Kylie's cards sell for about 75 cents. They also make giant cards on posterboard that sell for $2.50.

START-UP #73: YARD CARDS

It is becoming very popular to celebrate holidays and special events by displaying banners, announcements, or signs in front of your house. The most common examples are Christmas and New Year's greetings. But more and more frequently, we are seeing yards decorated for Easter, Halloween, Fourth of July, and other holidays. Yard signs and banners are also popular for birthdays, graduations and anniversaries, and to announce new births.

Energetic young entrepreneurs can take advantage of this decorating trend by starting a business that specializes in yard cards, signs, or banners for year-round occasions.

Some of the services you might offer:

Rental signs for special occasions

Air-brushed banners and announcements

Yard figures or scenes (painted on plywood)

Signs with greeting card messages

Garage sale signs or team support signs

Door or window signs for apartments

How to get started:

Make signs for your own yard, and start displaying them at every opportunity. Have flyers ready to hand out when neighbors comment on your unique signs or banners. Go through the neighborhood handing out flyers a few weeks before holidays or special community events. Then go back a few days later and visit homes with a sample book showing pictures of signs you've made. Once a few people start using your signs, your business will quickly multiply.

START-UP #74: CALLIGRAPHY

Calligraphy is the art of writing in fancy or elegant lettering styles. You can learn calligraphy by taking a class at a community center, reading books, and spending lots of time practicing. The only materials needed are a set of calligraphy pens and high-quality paper. Experienced calligraphers earn $10 to $35 an hour for their work.

How to get started:

1. If you know how to do calligraphy and want to start a business, begin your marketing by making signs or flyers advertising your services and having business cards printed.

2. Then make a portfolio or sample book of invitations, announcements, name cards, menus, signs, certificates, or gift items you can offer customers.

3. Visit local print shops, craft stores, office supply stores, and trophy shops to show the owners or managers your portfolio. Ask if you can leave flyers for customers who may be looking for a calligrapher.

4. Use your talent to hand-letter poems or verses on parchment paper (you must use copyright-free verses). Then frame and sell your work in gift shops, boutiques, or craft fairs.

5. Advertise in bridal shops or bridal magazines that you do hand-lettered invitations or announcements. Don't worry if customers don't live nearby. They will bring the work to you.

START-UP #75: DESIGNER T-SHIRTS

A T-shirt business is one of today's favorite businesses for young entrepreneurs. Julie Neubauer, age 17, who lives in Friendswood, Texas, started a T-shirt business when she was in fourth grade. She got interested in T-shirts when a friend suggested they take a class at a craft store. After the class, Julie practiced what she had learned by making T-shirts for birthday gifts. Her grandmother liked the shirt she made so much that Julie decided to start a business called Julie's Crafty T's.

T-shirts with iron-on appliqués:

Although there are dozens of ways to decorate T-shirts, Julie uses iron-on appliqués that she makes from various fabrics and outlines with paint pens. When she first started, it took about 2 hours to create one T-shirt. She now completes a T-shirt in 45 minutes or less.

Most of Julie's T-shirts are one-of-a-kind designs or custom orders. She has found that rich, bright colors and pictures of tropical fish, birds, and flowers sell best. She also sells a lot of Christmas T-shirts with Santas, reindeer, holly, and poinsettias. For the Fourth of July, she decorates shirts with teddy bears holding red, white, and blue flags. Julie says a custom-designed T-shirt costs about $8 to make and sells for $15 to $18.

Silk-screened T-shirts:

Bikini Shifaw, also age 17, of Washington, D.C., started a T-shirt business called Shifaw Shirts a year ago. He makes up about five designs for T-shirts, then takes customer surveys at school to determine which ones will sell best. Bikini is careful about choosing designs because it costs $17 to have each of his T-shirts silk-screened. He sells the shirts for $25 each.

Bikini recently won First Place in a business plan competition sponsored by the National Foundation for Teaching Entrepreneurship (NFTE). His prize was $1,000 for the start-up of his business. He was also selected by NFTE for the 1994 Young Entrepreneur of the Year award. Bikini is now in the process of revising his business plan and deciding the best ways to use the start-up money. One of his plans is to add baseball caps and team sports uniforms to his product line.

How to get started:

1. Specialize in one type of T-shirt (Examples: Tie-dyed, painted, air brushed). Visit craft stores to price materials and get ideas.

2. Experiment with designs and start developing your style.

3. Once you hit on a unique idea, make a sample shirt and wear it to school, shopping, or anywhere you go.

4. When people ask you to make a T-shirt, quote a fixed price that covers the supplies and at least $5 to $7 for your labor.

5. To keep from having to invest in blank T-shirts, ask your customers to supply their own prewashed shirt.

6. As you get more money to invest in supplies, make a bunch of shirts to sell in craft shows or door-to-door.

7. Look for small shops or boutiques that will display and sell your shirts in return for a percentage of the sales price.

8. Expand your business by making T-shirts for sports teams, dance groups, employee clubs, or special events.

Suggestions for success:

Julie Neubauer recommends providing care instructions for your T-shirt creations. She uses her computer to print instructions that say, "Wash inside out on gentle cycle. Dry on low heat." She safety-pins her business card and care instructions to the tag on each shirt.

·15·

How to Make Money with Your Special Talent

IS THERE SOMETHING YOU DO EASIER OR FASTER THAN EVERYONE ELSE? SOME subject you understand better than most other people your age or older? Something you love to do as much as you enjoy eating and breathing? If these questions make you think of a specific activity, hobby, or field of interest, you should pay careful attention. There is a great likelihood that you have a special talent for this activity.

Talented young people often do not recognize how amazing and gifted they are. What they do seems so easy, they think anyone can do it. If you are one of these young people, I hope you will take a closer look at yourself. How many people do you know who actually can perform at the level you have reached? If you are achieving unusual success for someone your age, it is likely you are talented.

Many young people think of a talented person as someone who can sing or dance, play a musical instrument, act, or write poetry. But talents are not always so traditional. You may have a talent for riding horses, fixing hair, building sand castles, or jumping ramps on a dirtbike. Don't put your talent down because it's different. Every talent you have should be recognized, cherished, and developed.

The happiest people are those who recognize their talents, capitalize on them, and make a career doing what they love. Young entrepreneurs have a special opportunity to develop their talents at an early age through starting a business enterprise. The 16 start-ups described in this chapter will give many examples of ways to explore your talent now.

Advantages of a business based on a special talent:

1. You get paid to do what you love. It doesn't seem like work.

2. Your natural talent gives you an edge over your competitors in the field.

3. Special skills usually command higher pay. Your opportunity for income is very promising.

4. You can explore career possibilities and make career achievements while you're very young.

Disadvantages of a business based on a special talent:

1. Age restrictions in your field can be frustrating. Sometimes the only way to overcome being young is to wait to grow older.

2. Transportation is often a problem. (You may be old enough to program a computer but too young to drive.) It's no fun asking your parents to drive you to your job.

3. It can be expensive to develop your talent. Not having enough money for equipment or training can be a roadblock to your goals.

OVERCOMING OBSTACLES

Creative people with special talents almost always have to overcome great obstacles to succeed. Some are laughed at and ridiculed for their ideas. Some are told by the experts that their plans will never work. Some are rejected by their peers and considered completely incompetent.

1. Milo Farnsworth, inventor of the first operating television, was thought to be a dangerous kook who should be treated with caution because he talked about the unknown idea of transmitting pictures with sound.

2. Ted Turner, founder of CNN, was told by his employees, industry leaders, and closest advisors that he was crazy to attempt a global 24-hour news cable network. Ten years later, people all over the world—including President Bush, Mikhail Gorbachev, and even Saddam Hussein—were watching CNN to find out what was happening in the Gulf War.

3. One of Ted Turner's favorite sayings is, "If you never quit, you're never beaten." Young people who are

successful pursue their dreams regardless of obstacles. If you want to be above average, follow the example of Thomas Edison, who said, "I never quit until I get what I want."

START-UP #76: MOBILE DISK JOCKEY

Steven Jay Shecter, age 13, who lives in Bayside, New York, started his business, Steven Jay Enterprises, when he was 7 years old. After attending a party and watching a mobile disk jockey perform, Steven knew he wanted to be a DJ more than anything else in the world. And he was determined to do it now, not when he was older.

At age 7, Steven started hosting dance parties for his friends in the basement music room of his home. Steven was the DJ. He had a microphone, a small cassette player, a few lights, some dance music, and a lot of enthusiasm. The kids thought the parties were great fun, but Steven knew this was just the beginning of what he would achieve.

Today, Steven owns about $5,000 in equipment and is able to offer full DJ service, professional lighting, and special effects. His flyers say, "We're more than just music. We make you feel like dancin'!"

Tips for success:

Steven's average fee for a school party, temple party, or Sweet-16 party is $300. When he books a party, he always requires a signed contract and a deposit. Then he works up a schedule for the party which includes special events, dances, lighting, breaks, and requested music. He hires dancers and an assistant for the evening and orders plenty of party favors such as inflatable mikes and guitars, bandannas, and Hawaiian leis. He also prepares his equipment, buys extra batteries for mikes, and refills the fog machine.

Since Steven doesn't drive yet, his parents transport all the equipment in the family van. After the party, Steven always pays his workers first, then all his bills for supplies, before he takes any money for himself. Most of his profit is reinvested in the business.

How to get started:

To get started in the DJ business today, Steven recommends the following equipment: two CD players, an amp, a mixing board, two speakers, stands, and a mike. He estimates the cost would be about $2,000 for a start-up. To be a success in this business, Steven says you have to care about what you do. "We don't just do it for the money," he says. "We do it because we enjoy it. The business is lots of fun!"

START-UP #77: FOREIGN-LANGUAGE TUTOR

If you are fortunate enough to speak a foreign language fluently, you have a highly desireable marketable skill. Here are some ways to earn money with your talent:

Offer private or group lessons for children. Parents today are very aware of the need to know more than one language.

Offer to speak in school classrooms or day care centers for a small fee. Show pictures or slides of your native country, talk about native foods and crafts, and teach the class five or six basic phrases used in everyday life.

Contact large corporations and offer language and etiquette classes for corporate representatives who travel or deal with foreign markets.

Offer businesses or private individuals your services as a translator.

START-UP #78: HOBBY INSTRUCTOR

Katie Finch, age 17, of Grants Pass, Oregon, is an accomplished pianist. Last year she worked as an apprentice to her piano teacher for 6 months to learn the Suzuki method of piano instruction. She now has four private students of her own. Since Katie is a new teacher, she charges only $4 per 30-minute lesson. Katie has enjoyed her teaching experience so much that she intends to teach music as a career.

If you have a skill in almost any hobby and enjoy teaching others, being a private instructor is an ideal business for you. Depending on your level of skill, you should be able to earn anywhere from $5 to $15 an hour helping others learn your craft. These are some of the lessons in great demand today: music lessons, cooking, cheerleading, twirling, clowning, juggling, dance, sewing, arts and crafts, makeup, hair braiding, and computer skills.

Bonus idea: Community education classes

Julie Neubauer, owner of Julie's Crafty T's, has been teaching classes on how to make T-shirts since she was 13. Julie started her class by talking to the director of the community education center at the local high school. The class is advertised through announcements sent out by the community center. The center handles all the registrations, and students are required to bring their own T-shirts. Julie teaches two 1 ½-hour sessions and makes about $40 to $50 for her time.

START-UP #79: STUDY BUDDY

When students need help, teachers often advise parents to hire a coach or tutor. If you are a good student, you can earn money helping other kids in the subjects that are easy for you.

How to get started:

Concentrate on working with kids just a few years younger than you. They will like the idea of a study partner rather than a tutor.

Hand out flyers to teachers and counselors at school. They will tell parents about you.

Advertise on bulletin boards at church or community organizations. Send notices to local newsletters.

How to work with students:

1. Set a schedule for working together each week. Twice a week for 1 hour is a good idea.

2. Agree with the parents on your pay. Adult tutors normally earn $12 to $15 an hour. You should be able to charge at least $8 per hour.

3. Stick to your study schedule. Start on time and end on time. A clock nearby will remind you.

4. Parents should be able to tell you where the student needs help and where to start. Teachers will also give suggestions.

5. Try to find ways to make studying fun. Offer small rewards. Make games. Use funny reminders. Praise any improvement.

START-UP #80: MURAL PAINTER

Wall murals are the latest trend in home decorating. If you are a good artist, you may enjoy creating scenes for children's bedrooms or playrooms.

A good way to get ideas is to attend model home shows held by local builders several times a year. These are some examples of paintings you may see:

Colorful hot-air balloons

Noah's ark with all the animals

Scenes from Star Trek (for a Trekkie fan)

A closet painted like a phone booth

Baseball scenes

Flower gardens

Alice in Wonderland scenes

How to get started:

To advertise yourself as a muralist, you will need a portfolio of pictures of your paintings. You can start by painting a mural in your own bedroom and taking pictures of the finished product. (It would be a good idea to ask your parents' permission first.) If you want to practice more, just paint over the mural with primer and a good coat of latex wall paint. When it's dry, you can start another mural.

When you propose a mural for a children's bedroom, you will need to show the customer a color sketch of what you plan to paint. Sometimes customers know exactly what they want, but many times you will have to interview the family to get ideas about their interests and hobbies. It is a good idea to ask each client to sign a written contract describing the work you will do. Most muralists also require a deposit of at least one-third down.

START-UP #81: FACE PAINTER

With a little practice on willing friends and family, almost anyone with artistic or creative ability can learn to do face painting. You also need to like being close to people. Being successful at running a face-painting booth or table in a festival, fair, or flea market requires an outgoing personality that attracts customers. If you have these talents, face painting pays very well.

Kristen Cox is 12 years old and lives in Houston, Texas. When she was in fifth grade, she decided she could earn some money face painting at the park in her subdivision. Here's how Kristen operated her business:

1. First, Kristen made an album showing 30 pictures she could paint. They were very simple drawings of things like dragons, clowns, smiley faces, flowers, rainbows, Ninja Turtles, and sail boats.

2. Then Kristen went to the park and told all the kids she would be there to face-paint tomorrow (Saturday).

3. The next day, Kristen and her brother, Austin (age 8), packed their red wagon with all the supplies they needed. They had a small table, two chairs, an umbrella, the paint supplies, and an ice chest with Koolaid to sell.

4. Kristen and Austin pulled the wagon down to the park and set up their table. They put up a sign that said "Face Painting by Kristen Cox."

5. Kristen used water-soluble artists' crayons to paint designs on faces, hands, and arms. Small pictures were 25 cents, and large pictures were 50 cents. Glitter was extra. Most of the designs could be painted in 2 to 3 minutes.

6. Austin painted faces for some of the little kids, but his job was mostly to sell Koolaid for 25 cents a cup.

7. Together, Kristen and Austin made $10, which they split equally. Since then, Kristen has done more face painting for birthday parties and at the school fair.

START-UP #82: MUSICAL PERFORMER

If you have a talent for singing or playing a musical instrument, there are many opportunities to market your skills. However, the music industry is extremely competitive, and you must be willing to work hard to achieve a reputation as a top performer.

Being a success in the music business requires two talents: (1) musical talent and (2) marketing talent. You have to be tops in your field of music, and you have to know how to tell other people about it.

How to market your talent:

First, decide what kind of music you specialize in. Then identify your target market. Focus your marketing efforts on those who are most interested in your music.

Best markets for rock bands are school parties or dances, private parties, special events for businesses that cater to teens, and teen clubs.

If you are a singer, jazz pianist, or have a small ensemble, restaurants and hotels will be the place to market your services.

An accomplished classical or religious musician might concentrate on doing weddings or performing in churches or synagogues. Weddings are usually paid, but church performances are often for love offerings.

Music is a public relations business. Join clubs and organizations where you will meet the kind of people who like your music. When the organization puts on an event, offer to provide some of the entertainment. Make sure a press release about your performance gets in the local papers. Follow up on every contact and referral you get. Above all, never give up. The next person you meet could be your lucky break.

START-UP #83: CLOWN

A clown is an actor who specializes in making people laugh at silly things. If you like to dress funny, pull pranks, and be the life of the party, you will enjoy clowning. Professional clowns today earn $60 to $80 an hour. You should be able to start out at $5 to $10 an hour and earn a great deal more as you get experience.

How to get started:

1. Take a class in clowning at a local community center. Or join a clowning group that performs in hospitals and nursing homes. These groups often give clowning lessons for free.

2. Develop your clown character. Decide on a costume and makeup. Get ideas from magazines and books on clowning. The most inexpensive costumes are homemade.

3. Work up some short clown routines that include balloon tricks, magic, jokes, juggling, mime, gymnastic stunts, or dance. To get experience, perform for children's groups at no charge.

4. Pass out colorful flyers in your neighborhood offering to appear at birthday parties or family events.

5. Give free performances at libraries or civic clubs to get your name out in the community. Hand out business cards and free balloons everywhere you go.

6. Market your clown services to restaurants, grocery stores, malls, or any business where parents take children. A regular Saturday clown should help their sales.

7. Make your sales calls in costume, just to show customers how much attention a clown can bring their business.

To learn more about clownmanship, read *Be a Clown!* by Turk Pipkin (Workman Publishing).

START-UP #84: COMPUTER CONSULTANT

Computer businesses are a fascinating and challenging field full of opportunity for young entrepreneurs. If you know how to write programs, customize software, or solve computer problems, your services will be in high demand. People who need your help won't care how old you are, whether you can drive, or what you look like. They just need someone who understands computers.

Success story: MediClaim software

Jeremy Mattern, age 17, and Brian Wood, age 15, live in Sugar Land, Texas. They became friends in elementary school because of their mutual interest in computers and entrepreneurship. Today they are partners in a business called MediClaim, which files insurance claims for doctors by computer. Brian is the manager of software development. Jeremy is director of marketing.

Brian says he learned to program in Pascal during third grade by studying a manual in his spare time. Jeremy learned to program at an early age also. The two boys have been developing computer programs together since that time. In junior high, they named their business Desktop Software Company. That business name is still used to process orders from customers who want to pay by credit card.

According to Brian, Jeremy has a talent for asking questions and always being where interesting things happen. Jeremy is the one who got the idea for the MediClaim software one day last year while visiting with his dentist. He immediately told Brian, and the two of them developed the design for MediClaim. Brian wrote the program, while Jeremy researched ways to market and sell it to doctors.

Marketing methods:

Jeremy conducted phone surveys of doctors to find out what claim-filing system they were using and what they would be willing to pay for a claim service. Once they found out the going rate, Jeremy and Brian set the price of their software low enough to be competitive. Then Jeremy faxed one-page ads about MediClaim to all the doctor's offices. They also designed a professional brochure that gives details about the claim-filing service. For a copy of their brochure, write to P.O. Box 734, Sugar Land, TX 77487.

Suggestions for success:

In addition to filing claims by computer, Jeremy and Brian can file paper claims when necessary. They also generate and mail monthly statements for doctors. When a doctor subscribes to their service, Jeremy goes to the doctor's office to install the software and train the office personnel how to use it.

Doctors pay an initial software charge, a monthly service charge, and a processing fee for each claim. Brian has written software that bills each doctor's office monthly for the services they have received. Jeremy and Brian don't have any problems with late payments since Jeremy enacted a late-fee policy that requires doctors to pay extra if they are 30 days late paying their account.

The next step Jeremy and Brian plan is to incorporate their business under the name DataCorp. There will be several other divisions of the business besides MediClaim. Research and development continues as Jeremy and Brian pursue their ultimate goal of one day inventing new computer technology.

START-UP #85: DESKTOP PUBLISHING

If you have a good eye for design, have access to a computer and laser printer, and know how to use some good software programs for publishing, you can start a desktop-publishing business. These are some services you can offer:

    Typing resumes, letters, or research papers

    Maintaining mailing lists

    Printing labels and form letters

    Sending and receiving fax transmissions

Designing menus or programs for events

Making custom greeting cards for all occasions

Printing party invitations and birth announcements

Making signs for trade shows and garage sales

Designing flyers and business cards

Producing brochures, price lists, or business forms

Most desktop-publishing experts charge at least $25 an hour. You should be able to start out charging $15 an hour and make a very nice income with this business.

How to get started:

Make a portfolio of sample cards, invitations, letters, and signs you can create. Then design a flyer advertising your services and listing some of your prices. Distribute your flyers to small business owners, churches, teachers, and students. Try to set up appointments to show your portfolio and discuss your customer's desktop-publishing needs.

Success story: MelMaps

Melissa Gollick, age 11, of Denver, Colorado, started her computer graphics company when she was in third grade. However, she has been interested in computers since preschool. One of the reasons she likes computers so much is, "The computer doesn't know if you are a boy or girl. It treats you just the same."

Melissa, nicknamed Mel, got the idea for a business called MelMaps by listening to her dad, who is a real estate consultant, talking to a client. They were discussing location maps and how much the client had to pay a graphics design company to produce them. Melissa said she could make the map for free.

The next day, Melissa showed the client a sample map. Since that time, this client has bought over 200 maps from her. Melissa's average fee for a location or vicinity map is $20 to $50. She also makes floor plans and site maps for $50 to $100 each. Her best clients are realtors, appraisers, banks, home buyers, and anyone trying to tell out-of-town guests how to find their home or business.

During her first year in business, Melissa was chosen by Young Americans Bank in Denver as Young Entrepreneur of the Year. Her prize was $250 start-up money and free business cards. She was also a finalist in the competition for Rocky Mountain

Entrepreneur of the Year. Melissa says that was fun, even though she didn't win. Young Americans Bank escorted Melissa and her parents to the awards ceremony in a big limo.

START-UP #86: FREELANCE WRITER

If you enjoy writing mysteries, short stories, science fiction, plays, poetry, political commentary, news reports, profiles of famous people, or how-to articles, you may enjoy a business as a freelance writer. Your job will be to sell your writing to newspapers, magazines, or book publishers who are always looking for creative new ideas.

How to get started:

1. Practice your craft. The way to get good at writing is to write. Many writers use a journal for this purpose.

2. Ask your librarian where to find back issues of *Writer's Digest Magazine*. These magazines are full of helpful articles on how to become a better writer.

3. Read books on freelance writing recommended by *Writer's Digest Magazine*. If you can't afford to buy the books, borrow them from the library.

4. Ask the library to get the book *Market Guide for Young Writers* by Kathy Henderson. This book tells how to submit your work to publishers. It also gives mailing addresses.

5. Make it your goal to get published somewhere. Write for the school newspaper or a church or community newsletter. You won't get paid, but you may get a by-line.

6. Enter writing contests and attend meetings of local writer's groups.

7. Selling your writing is a business. You have to keep sending out work regularly if you want a regular income. Once you sell your first piece, the next ones will come much easier.

START-UP #87: NEWSLETTER PUBLISHING

Newsletters are small publications that provide news and information interesting only to a particular group of readers. Examples are neighborhood newsletters, PTA newsletters, church newsletters, arts and crafts newsletters, or home schooling newsletters.

How to make money with newsletters:

1. Advertise your services as a newsletter writer and editor. Groups that are too busy to write their own newsletter will pay you to do the work.

2. Publish a newsletter full of local news about schools, sports, entertainment, restaurants, civic groups, and social events. Sell single issues throughout the neighborhood, or sell yearly subscriptions.

3. Publish a newsletter that is distributed free in a specific area of town. Sell advertising space to businesses that want to reach these readers. You can also sell ad space to readers who want to sell household items or advertise garage sales.

4. Publish a free newsletter about a specific topic such as arts and crafts, gardening, or entertainment. Make your money by selling other products through the newsletter, such as books, hobby supplies, patterns and instructions, tools, or personalized gift items.

Success story: Heavenly Highlights

Katie Finch, age 17, of Grants Pass, Oregon, has published a small newsletter she calls *Heavenly Highlights Magazine* since she was 12. The monthly 5 1/2-inch × 8 1/2-inch publication averages 16 pages an issue and costs $10 a year for a subscription. The purpose of the magazine is to publish children's writing and art. Most of the writers are home schoolers. Katie produces the newsletter on her home computer and has about 100 subscribers. For information, write Katie Finch, 345 E. Hawksdale Drive, Grants Pass, OR 97526.

Success story: Global Teen Club International

Cathryn Murray, age 19, of Walnut Creek, California, (the same Cathryn Murray who had the candy business in Chapter 1), started publishing the Global Teen Club newsletter when she was 14. Like Katie Finch, Cathryn wanted a way to help other young people get their writing and art published. Today, Cathryn's newsletter has 500 teen subscribers from countries all over the world.

As editor of the Global Teen Club newsletter, Cathryn gets 10 to15 letters a day from teens responding to articles in the newsletter or submitting work they hope to get published. Cathryn works from an office in her bedroom, answering all the letters personally and producing the newsletter on an old computer donated by a local business.

No one's work is ever rejected. However, it does take time for Cathryn to work through the backlog of submissions and get everyone's articles printed. Subjects covered in the newsletter include world events, self-esteem, violence, AIDS, rape, disabilities, stamp collecting, poetry, book reviews, and art. Cathryn says some of her writers have been sending work for 4 years. She is very proud to say she sees a remarkable improvement in their writing skills.

The ten-page Global Teen Club newsletter costs $600 a month to publish. Subscriptions are $8 for 6 months. However, many of the teens in Third World countries cannot pay at all. Rather than drop them from the list, Cathryn pays for their issues out of her own pocket. In addition to attending school full time, Cathryn works three part-time jobs to support the newsletter and pay her living expenses. She and her mother live on Cathryn's income and a small monthly disability check her mother receives.

Last year, Cathryn attended a 1-week training camp called Camp Enterprise, sponsored by An Income of Her Own (a business training organization for girls). Cathryn learned a lot more about how to make her newsletter a successful business enterprise. She is currently working on a business plan and looking for grant money to support the Global Teen Club. She envisions her newsletter developing into a full-scale magazine that will be sold on newsstands throughout the world. Subscriptions may be sent to Cathryn Murray, 3120 Oak Road, Suite 309, Walnut Creek, CA 94596.

START-UP #88: VIDEO PRODUCER

If you have access to a video camera, you can start a business producing short how-to videos on almost any subject. Tapes should be no longer than 15 to 30 minutes each and may cover topics such as these:

How to change a flat tire on your bike

How to buy a used car

How to train your dog to do tricks

How to make real Italian lasagna

How to tie-dye a T-shirt

You can find out what subjects will sell best by taking surveys in your neighborhood. When you discover a subject a lot of people want to know about, research the topic and produce the video.

Say, for example, you want to produce a video on tie-dying T-shirts. The local craft store owner will be happy to share information for the video because more customers will come to his store to buy supplies.

Since your videos will be homemade, you will not have the overhead expenses of a professional publisher. You can charge less for your videos and still make a nice profit for your time.

START-UP #89: SPORTS COACH

Young people or children who are trying to learn a new sport often need a lot of individual help. Busy parents today don't have as much time to help children practice basic skills. If you like sports and enjoy children, advertise your services as a private sports coach. You can give private or group coaching in softball, baseball, soccer, volleyball, basketball, football, track, tennis, golf, or whatever sport you excel in. Besides earning money, your own skills will improve as you teach others.

Success story: Jolie's Riding School

Jolie Barras of Friendswood, Texas, has loved horses since she was a little girl. She started riding when she was 3. By age 4, she was winning ribbons and trophies in shows while competing against kids as old as 14. However, she never took any riding lessons until she was in junior high.

In high school, Jolie started barrel racing. Then, during her senior year, she worked as an assistant to her riding teacher. She earned $5 an hour helping the kids, saddling horses, brushing the horses, and cleaning stables. During this time, Jolie learned a lot about how to teach riding.

Right after Jolie graduated from high school, her dad asked her to give a few riding lessons to the 10-year-old son of his best friend's secretary. Jolie enjoyed it so much, she decided she wanted to teach full time. She named her business Jolie's Riding School.

To get students, Jolie made flyers and brochures and distributed them everywhere. Although she was only 18, Jolie joined the Chamber of Commerce and started attending meetings. She made a magnetic sign for her truck and posted signs along the roads leading to her property.

Today, Jolie has been in business for 2 years. She currently has 55 students, 8 horses, and 11 saddles. Her barn is on 15 acres that she is buying. She owns a 1989 Chevy pickup, a three-horse trailer, a flatbed trailer, and a John Deere tractor. She's certified to teach both English and western riding on the intermediate level by the Camp Horsemanship Association, located in Hunt, Texas.

With all this success, people still ask how old she is when they see her at the Chamber of Commerce luncheons. "They can hardly believe I'm the owner of a business," laughs Jolie. "To them, I look 13, but I'm determined to prove I can do well."

START-UP #90: INVENTOR

Many people think inventors are wiry-haired old men who spend all their time in laboratories. The truth is most inventors are ordinary people who see creative solutions to common problems. This book contains the stories of several young inventors:

> Larry Villella invented the ConServ Sprinkler because he got tired of watering the shrubs in front of his house (Chapter 7).

> David Kahl, Jr. invented *Better Letters* to help young people write letters for all occasions (start-up #50). (Note: David's book is an invention because of the unique notebook he designed for it. He won on inventing contest with it.)

> Keeya Branson created a new type of jewelry made from discarded copper wire and telephone wire (start-up #71).

> Jeremy Mattern and Brian Wood invented the MediClaim system to file insurance claims for doctors (start-up #84).

The inventing process:

According to Alan Tratner, president of Inventors Workshop International, the most important thing you can do when you have an idea for an invention is to write it down. He advises all young inventors to keep a notebook with careful records, drawings, and notes about their ideas. Each entry should be signed and dated. As additional evidence, have a friend witness your journal entries and sign them also.

The next step is to build a prototype (model) of your invention. Larry and David used things around the house to make samples of their inventions. This process helps you improve the invention. When you are satisfied with the prototype, you can show it to trusted friends and relatives. Ask them for a written evaluation of the invention. Their letters are additional proof that you are the inventor.

Next, you will need to decide how to manufacture and market the invention. Keeya simply made samples of her jewelry and started selling them. David took his prototype of *Better Letters* to printers for quotes. Once he had a final copy of the book, David protected his invention by getting it copyrighted. Larry is still in the process of trying to get a patent on the ConServ Sprinkler. For the first year, he manufactured the sprinklers in his basement. Today the sprinklers are manufactured and distributed by a company Larry found to take over the job.

Inventors are almost always entrepreneurs who promote and market their own products. To learn more about the inventing and patenting process, write to the Inventors Workshop International, 7332 Mason Avenue, Canoga Park, CA 91306.

START-UP #91: ACTOR AND BROADCASTER

Radio and TV shows with teen and pre-teen reporters and interviewers are becoming more popular across the United States. The chances of a young person's landing a regular spot as a show host are increasing daily. If you have talents in acting, writing, or broadcasting, you can start developing a career now while you are young.

Evan Roberts, age 11, of East Rockaway, New York, began his career as a sportscaster, radio personality, and actor over 2 years ago. His first big break was being selected as a cast member on a cable TV show called *Dynamets*, which is a weekly kids' show about the New York Mets baseball team.

Evan's assignments included interviewing players, announcing play-by-play with Rusty Staub and Howie Rose, and answering baseball trivia questions.

Last year, Evan hosted a weekly hour-long radio show on WGBB-1240 AM called *Kids Sports Talk*. On this program, Evan interviewed sports celebrities and invited kids to call in and discuss their viewpoint on sports. He has also done a number of voice-overs for radio commercials and acted in educational videos.

Another of Evan's interests is stand-up comedy. He not only won the "Funniest Kid Contest" held at a well-known comedy club in Manhattan but also was asked to sign a contract to host future kid contests at the club. He has also been approached by a group looking for someone to announce wrestling matches. Although Evan's career goal is to be a sportscaster, he will announce anything to get experience.

Evan has been interviewed on *Live with Regis and Kathie Lee* (on ABC) and featured on *A Current Affair* (Fox Broadcasting). Evan also writes a monthly sports column for a Long Island publication called *Island Kids and Parents*.

This is Evan's advice for a young person who wants a career in any type of broadcasting:

1. Start now developing your skills and style. Evan started announcing around the house when he was as young as 5 years old. His dad, who wanted to be a sportscaster when he was young, coached Evan on techniques.

2. Study the masters in your field. Evan listens to all-sports radio almost constantly to keep up with sports events and learn from other sports announcers.

3. Become an expert in your field. Evan reads at least one newspaper every day and sometimes three. He also memorizes sports facts from a sports encyclopedia on his computer.

4. Practice your writing skills. News commentators and broadcasters often have to write their own material.

5. Build your vocabulary. Evan works especially hard to learn new adjectives and big words that describe things.

·16·

How to Cash in on Holidays

WITH GOOD PLANNING, YOU CAN MAKE MONEY ON HOLIDAYS ALL YEAR LONG. ALMOST every month of the year has a holiday or special event to be celebrated. Use a calendar to plan your holiday enterprises at least 3 months in advance. Give yourself plenty of time to order supplies, make costumes, create an inventory to sell, and get signed up for craft shows and festivals. Once customers find out you specialize in being prepared for holidays, they will start calling you first whenever they need a holiday gift or service.

* Holiday Calendar *

Advantages of a holiday business:

1. Celebrating holidays is fun. With a holiday business, you get to start the season earlier and enjoy it longer.

2. People spend lots of money at holidays. It's fairly easy to sell when everyone is in the mood to buy.

3. Almost everyone has extra work during the holidays. If you provide a service that helps busy people save time, you will get a lot of business.

4. You can never run out of holiday ideas. For months before every holiday, magazines and newspapers are crammed with ideas for holiday crafts, cooking, and decorating. You will have plenty of fuel for creative thinking.

Disadvantages of a holiday business:

1. You have to plan ahead. You can't wait until a week before the holiday and decide to start a business.

2. Holiday businesses have time limits. The time to make money is while the season is in full swing. When it's over, you don't want a lot of leftover inventory.

3. Competition is high during the holidays. Lots of other businesses will be advertising and running sales also. Your customers will expect a bargain.

Holiday marketing

Besides the ten holiday start-ups outlined in this chapter, many of the businesses suggested throughout this book will do very well during holiday seasons, particularly those involving crafts, food, and retail sales. Smart entrepreneurs always watch the holiday calendar and plan ways to cash in on holidays.

If you want to know what your customers need or want at holidays, take a survey. Ask them how you can help them most during the next holiday. People love giving their opinion. Listen closely to what they say. They will tell you exactly how to direct your business for maximum profits in the next holiday season.

START-UP #92: CHRISTMAS DECORATING

Of all the holidays of the year, people spend the most time and money decorating for the December holidays of Christmas, Kwanza, and Hanukkah. The buying season for these decorations starts in early October. Most people have finished decorating their homes by the first week in December. However, they still buy decorations throughout the month of December for gifts or to add to their collections for next year.

Decorating items or services to sell:

1. Tree decorations are always in demand. Make mini-wreaths, clothespin reindeers, crocheted Santas, painted wood stars or stockings, fancy bows, ceramic figures, stuffed fabric gingerbread men, or garlands for the tree.

2. Many people today collect angels all year long. Create a series of angels and give them names and identities. Print up little cards to go with each one explaining what the name means.

3. Deliver miniature live Christmas trees decorated with tiny stars and lights for desk displays in offices.

4. Sell wreaths and door swags made out of greenery you have gathered free or almost free.

5. Gather mistletoe and sell it to caterers, decorators, or individuals. A small sprig is worth $1.

6. Make and sell holiday candles of all kinds.

7. Give classes on how to make a gingerbread house, holiday crafts, candles, or wreaths.

8. Make personalized Christmas stockings, aprons, mugs, or tree ornaments. Create holiday tree skirts, table cloths, wall hangings, or pillows.

Suggestions for success:

When the Christmas buying season gets in full swing, you need to be selling, not manufacturing, your products. Several months before the season begins, decide how much inventory you need. Then set a work schedule to make a certain number of items each week. It takes discipline to make Christmas ornaments in the summer, but you'll be glad you prepared for the holiday rush.

START-UP #93: GIFT WRAPPING

December is a busy time of the year. Everyone is shopping, decorating, baking, going to parties. What's the chore that busy people often leave undone until the last minute? Wrapping all the presents they've bought. This is the perfect time to start a gift-wrapping service.

How to get started:

1. *Get a plan.* Visit craft stores; browse through holiday magazines. Select several simple but attractive gift-wrapping designs you will offer.

2. *Gather supplies.* Buy paper, gift bags, ribbon, and bows on sale. Start saving boxes of all sizes and shapes.

3. *Make samples.* Wrap some empty boxes, so customers can see your designs and make choices.

4. *Create a price list.* Set rates according to the size of the package. Double your rate for hard-to-wrap items and specialty jobs. Offer special prices for customers who want to provide their own supplies and pay you by the hour.

5. *Advertise your service.* Make flyers and give them out to friends, neighbors, and relatives. Put notices on local bulletin boards. Look for businesses that will allow you to place flyers on their counter or in the window.

6. *Organize your work.* Keep a notebook with a special page for each customer. Write down all special instructions, the prices you agreed on, and deadlines for packages to be ready.

When your satisfied customers tell others about your service, you may become very busy. It is very important to keep up with your work every day. People are counting on you to help them get those gifts are under the tree before Santa arrives.

Bonus Idea: Gift wrapping for shops or stores

Ask owners of local shops or stores if you can have a gift-wrapping table in front of their store on a Saturday during the December shopping season. While you are earning extra money, you'll be helping the store promote goodwill. Your gift-wrapping service will also be appropriate for Valentine's Day and Mother's Day.

START-UP #94: HOLIDAY CHILD CARE

Good babysitters are in high demand during the holidays. In fact, the busiest night of the year for sitters is New Year's Eve. It's not unusual to earn double your normal hourly rate on this holiday.

If you like children and don't mind being busy on holidays, a holiday child care business may be right for you. These are some services you might provide:

Premium babysitting services for holiday occasions that are mostly for adults (New Year's Eve, Valentine's Day)

Saturday afternoon playgroups for children whose parents want to shop before a holiday

Group babysitting for churches, clubs, and organizations that have special holiday events

Overnight child care when parents go out of town

An excellent book that will help you plan a child care business is *Kid Sitter Basics* by Celeste Stuhring, R.N. (Westport Publishers, 1994).

START-UP #95: VALENTINE'S GIFTS

Valentine's Day is less than 8 weeks after Christmas. As soon as Christmas is over, you need to switch immediately into gear for Valentine's Day gifts. Check the after-Christmas clearance sales for lace, red ribbon, sequins, and other supplies you can use for Valentine's Day projects.

Suggestions for Valentine's Day gift items:

1. Decorating with hearts can turn almost anything into a Valentine's gift: balloons, stuffed animals, T-shirts, earrings, baskets, picture frames, a tiny plant, or a single rose.

2. Make and sell small craft items like refrigerator magnets or tiny decorated baskets of potpourri. An hour spent in a craft store will give you dozens of ideas. A sure bet: anything red and white, heart shaped, pretty, or perfumed.

3. Create one-of-a-kind, custom Valentine's cards on your computer or hand-decorate with stamp art, glitter, paper doilies, dried flowers, and ribbon. If you do calligraphy, write personalized Valentine messages in your cards.

4. Turn your kitchen skills into gifts. Take orders for homemade peanut brittle, fudge, caramel corn, baskets of muffins, decorated cookies, gourmet brownies, or low-calorie cheesecake for dieters.

A good book to read is *Potpourri, Incense and Other Fragrant Concoctions* by Ann Tucker Fettner (Workman Publishing). The book tells how to make your own potpourri, scented candles, sachets, and toilet water.

START-UP #96: COSTUMED CHARACTERS

Dressing up is not just for Halloween. Costume shops have costumes for just about any holiday of the year. If you enjoy acting, an ideal business for you is holiday character appearances.

Suggestions for characters:

New Year's Eve: Father Time

Valentine's Day: Cupid

St. Patrick's Day: Leprechaun

Easter: Easter Bunny

Fourth of July: Uncle Sam

Halloween: The Great Pumpkin

Christmas: Santa

How to get started:

1. Start planning 6 weeks before the holiday. Make your costume, or reserve one at a costume shop.

2. Advertise with flyers in your neighborhood. Offer a discount for those who call by a certain date. Require a deposit with the order.

3. Arrange fund-raisers for clubs or school groups. Pay the club a commission for taking orders for your visits or costumed gift deliveries.

4. Talk to store owners, restaurants, or places of entertainment. They may hire you to appear in costume and hand out candy or small gifts to customers.

5. Charge more for party appearances. Costumed visits are a big hit with children. You will need to develop a short routine of tricks and

gags. Plan to hand out inexpensive favors, and allow each child to have pictures taken with you.

If you need ideas for your act, read *Magic for Beginners* by Harry Baron (Prima Publishing). This book teaches over 75 professional magic tricks that beginners any age can learn and perform.

START-UP #97: ST. PATRICK'S DAY FAVORS

St. Patrick's Day has gained a lot of popularity in recent years. The symbol for this holiday is a green four-leaf clover. Young entrepreneurs can cash in on St. Patrick's Day by selling almost anything green.

Ways to help celebrate St. Patrick's Day:

1. Make and sell favors such as badges, buttons, pens, pencils, drink holders, balloons, or key chains with Irish sayings or four-leaf clovers.

2. Make items to wear, such as hats, aprons, vests, or T-shirts decorated for St. Patrick's Day.

3. Use green food colors with some of your favorite recipes to create green bakery items such as decorated cookies, cupcakes, candies, or breads.

4. Create and sell St. Patrick's Day centerpieces, door hangings, or wall decorations.

5. Get a group of friends together and learn Irish songs. Hire yourselves out to perform at restaurants around St. Patrick's Day.

START-UP #98: EASTER BASKET TREATS

Easter is the second largest holiday for gift buying of the whole year (Christmas is first). If you enjoy the Easter season, start a business that specializes in unusual favors or treats for Easter baskets.

Ideas for treats to make and sell:

1. Specialize in unusual or collectible Easter eggs. Craft books give suggestions for all kinds. Examples are ceramic eggs, blown eggs, hand-painted eggs, or confetti eggs.

2. Personalize plastic eggs with children's names. Fill with non-edible treats such as school erasers in animal shapes, tiny chicks made of pom-poms, or finger puppets.

3. Sell small, inexpensive craft items such as pipe-cleaner Easter bunnies, bean bags, little stuffed animals, or hair bows. Craft books will give you many more ideas.

4. Make Easter puppets in animal shapes. Give them names, and make up Easter stories to go with them.

5. Create gifts with religious themes. Popular items are bookmarks, crosses, jewelry, and framed Bible phrases.

Suggestions for success:

Easter is celebrated on different dates each year, but always sometime during March or April. Check your calendar for the correct date, and plan your work schedule at least 2 to 3 months in advance. If you sell personalized items, start taking orders at least 4 weeks before Easter.

START-UP #99: COSTUME FACTORY

If you like to sew, Halloween is the ideal time for you to start a business making costumes. You will need to start early in the summer designing your costumes and making samples. Create a portfolio of your costume ideas and start taking orders in September.

How to get started:

1. Get permission to turn your bedroom or basement into a temporary costume factory. Start collecting all kinds of items that can be used for costuming: old wigs, jewelry, hats, discarded clothing, and sewing materials.

2. Study pattern books at fabric stores for ideas. Buy a few basic patterns that can be altered to make a variety of costumes.

3. Collect ideas from craft books or books on costuming. You will find suggestions for using common things around the house such as paper plates, paper bags, cardboard boxes, old sheets, toilet paper tubes, construction paper, felt, and paper-mâché.

4. Offer customers a trade-in discount. Recycle outgrown or slightly damaged costumes into new costumes for someone else.

5. Create two or three one-size-fits-all costumes that you can mass produce fairly quickly. Price these lower than your made-to-fit costumes.

6. Made-to-fit and custom-ordered costumes will take longer and bring higher prices. Ask for a 50% deposit with the order, so that you have money to buy supplies. Schedule appointments for fittings 1 or 2 weeks before Halloween. Give yourself plenty of time for possible alterations or last- minute customers.

Bonus idea: Theatrical costumes

Costume designers are needed throughout the year for all kinds of theatrical and musical productions. If you enjoy the costuming business, offer your services to drama and music departments at high schools and colleges.

START-UP #100: NEW-PRODUCT ASSEMBLY

Holidays are traditional times to buy new bikes, exercise equipment, swing sets, trampolines, computers, and stereos. However, a lot of people don't have the patience or mechanical skills to assemble or install their new products. If you are the person at your house who always puts things together, consider starting a year-round business as a new-product assembly specialist.

How to get started:

GET IT
TOGETHER!

Call Pat
222-1122

1. Advertise your service with flyers distributed in the neighborhood just a few days before major gift-giving holidays.

2. Set your fees at about half the fee customers would pay for assembly or installation provided by the store.

3. Look for stores, bike shops, and salespeople who will give you referrals. Leave a supply of business cards with them. They will make more sales if they can tell customers where to get inexpensive installation.

4. Have stickers printed with your business name and phone number. Put one of your stickers on the side or back of every product

you assemble. Customers will be able to call you again for future assembly projects.

5. Offer customers who give you referrals a 10% discount on their next assembly job.

START-UP #101: HOLIDAY EMPORIUM

Having a retail store that must be open during traditional business hours is out of the question for young people in school. But what about a shop that only opens on special holidays, vacations, or just when you have time? With the right marketing, this idea can work very well. Several young entrepreneurs have already tried it.

Success venture: Fun Stuff

Last year, Gregory Collins and five friends in third and fourth grade started a business called Fun Stuff. The business operated for 6 weeks during the summer. It was located on a table setup on the sidewalk in downtown Lewes, Delaware. The space was provided by one of the mothers who owned a shop there.

The goal of the business was to sell "fun stuff" like beach toys, floats, squirt guns, sand pails, and games to tourists who visited their beaches. They were only open during what they considered "prime time" shopping hours, which was 10 AM to 2 PM on Thursdays, Fridays, Saturdays, and Sundays.

People in town thought the idea of a store run by grade school students was wonderful. Local papers ran a big story about the children, including pictures. Despite their limited hours, the business did very well, and Greg looks forward to running the store again next summer.

Success venture: Nick's Nacks

Nick Batchelor, an eighth-grader in Salida, Colorado, started a retail store called Nick's Nacks 2 years ago. Nick only opens the store for special 2-day sales on holidays. It is located in a 20-foot by 30-foot building next to the family's home and print shop on the edge of town.

Nick sells a wide variety of merchandise, much like the old general stores of days gone by. In the store, you can find almost anything from dolls to survival knives or jewelry designed by Nick. Much of the inventory comes from a store his grandfather once owned. Nick pays his grandfather 20 percent on these sales.

When a holiday nears, Nick cleans up the store (which gets dusty because of the dirt road) and puts out flyers in town advertising his special 2-day sale. Townspeople have come to enjoy shopping at the unusual emporium because Nick almost always has something new and different on the shelves. Kids who visit the store also get to pet the goats, rabbits, chickens, and ducks that run free on the property.

Nick gets ideas for new merchandise to put in his store by watching what customers buy at the truck stop where he buses tables several evenings a week. His advice for other young people is to "be patient while you're building a business." Nick has learned it takes time to build customer loyalty and create a successful business.

For sources of inventory for your holiday store, check *The Wholesale-by-Mail Catalog*, published every year by HarperCollins Publishers in New York. This book lists over 500 sources to shop by mail and receive 30-percent to 90-percent discount on products.

·17·

WHERE TO GET MORE
INFORMATION

STARTING A BUSINESS IS A PROCESS OF LEARNING. NO ONE EVER KNOWS EVERYTHING from the very beginning.

Successful entrepreneurs learn a little bit more every day. They read books, do research, ask for advice, take classes, attend workshops, talk to other business people, and join organizations where they can learn new methods of doing business well. If you want to be a success in your business, learning should never stop.

This chapter contains a listing of numerous resources you may consult to get more information. Research can be a very exciting process. One small detail you discover could make the difference between barely making a profit or becoming wildly successful.

ORGANIZATIONS TO CONTACT

National Foundation for Teaching Entrepreneurship (NFTE), Steve Mariotti, President, 64 Fulton Street, Suite 700, New York, NY 10038 (212-233-1777). This nonprofit organizaton offers comprehensive programs to train inner-city and disadvantaged youths in the basics of business and entrepreneurship. Young people who receive training by NFTE have a very high success rate in business because of their solid foundation of basic business skills. Request information on programs in your community or business materials you can purchase.

International Directory of Young Entrepreneurs (IDYE), Jennifer Kushell, Marketing Director, 3905 Lake Vista Court, Encino, CA 91316 (1-800-455-4393). Started by three college students, this is a worldwide networking organization for young entrepreneurs that provides a membership directory on a database and a quarterly newsletter. Members ranging in age from the early teens to the 30s endeavor to assist each other toward success in business. If you want to meet other young entrepreneurs, this is the organization for you.

Young Americans Bank, 311 Steele Street, Denver, CO 80206 (303-394-4357). This bank opened in 1987 to teach young people under 22 how to responsibly handle bank accounts through hands-on experience. Request information about banking by mail. They also give small loans to young people for business start-ups. Teachers may request information about Young AmeriTowne, a curriculum for teaching economics and free enterprise.

Junior Achievement, Inc., One Education Way, Colorado Springs, CO 80906 (719-540-8000). This is the oldest, largest, and fastest growing nonprofit organization in the world that exists for the purpose of teaching business and economics. Request information about groups meeting in your community. Teachers my request information about programs for grades K-12.

Kidz in Biz Productions, Enid J.H. Karpeh, Director, 115 W. 74th Street, New York, NY 10023 (212-787-7629). Request information about trade shows for young entrepreneurs held at various locations in the U.S.

Inventors Workshop International Education Foundation, Alan Tratner, President, 7332 Mason Avenue, Canoga Park, CA 91306 (818-340-4268). This organization offers many resources for young inventors and young entrepreneurs. Request information on educational programs that help inventors succeed and information on how to get a patent.

An Income of Her Own, Joline Godfrey, Director, P.O. Box 987, Santa Barbara, CA 93102 (1-800-350-2978). Request information about Camp Start-Up, an entrepreneurial skills-building summer camp for teen women.

The National Education Center for Women in Business (NECWB), Seton Hill College, Box 288-K, Seton Hill Drive, Greensburg, PA 15601 (1-800-NECWB-4U). This nonprofit organization has a camp for teenage girls in the summer called Camp Entrepreneurship.

They also publish a newsletter called *EntreVision* and have a catalog of business books and materials.

National 4-H Council, 7100 Connecticut Avenue, Chevy Chase, MD 20815 (301-961-2800). Request information about 4-H groups in your area and how to participate in activities. This organization also sponsors state and national entrepreneurship conferences for youth.

University-Community Outreach Program (UCOP), University of Pennsylvania, 1208 Steinberg Hall-Dietrich Hall, 3620 Locust Walk, Philadelphia, PA 19104 (610-668-5330). Request information about the Young Entrepreneurs Program at Wharton that teaches young people how to run their own businesses, provides mentors, and offers grants up to $500. This program is also offered at Columbia University and University of California at Berkeley.

SBA Small Business Answer Desk (1-800-827-5722). Open 9 AM to 5 PM Eastern Standard Time, Monday through Friday. Operators will answer basic business questions and refer callers to appropriate Small Business Administration (SBA) offices for more help.

Free Enterprise Fund for Children, Attn: Mark Victor Hansen, P.O. Box 7665, Newport Beach, CA 92658. Request applications and information about grants to help young people start businesses.

Business Kids, 301 Almeria Avenue, Suite 330, Coral Gables, FL 33134 (1-800-852-4544). Ask for information about *The Business Kit* that helps young entrepreneurs plan and start a business. This company also sells numerous Business Kid products such as T-shirts, stationery, tapes, and videos.

Leading Education Equation (LEE), *Inc.,* 11 Esopus Avenue, Kingston, NY 12401 (914-331-3978). This youth organization helps young people learn business skills, job skills, video skills, and computer skills. Ask for information about career training and college preparation programs.

Homeland Publications, 2615 Calder Drive, Dept. 3, League City, TX 77573 (713-332-9764). Request information about *Kids Business* software program created by Bonnie Drew to help beginning entrepreneurs run a business successfully. Teachers may request information about school programs presented by Bonnie Drew, author of *Fast Cash for Kids.*

FURTHER READING
Books on general business and financial topics

How to Become a Teenage Millionaire, by Todd Temple. Teen's guide to making, saving, and spending money wisely. Written with a sense of humor (Thomas Nelson Publishers, Nashville, TN, 1991).

The Teenage Entrepreneur's Guide, by Sarah L. Riehm. Detailed explanation of 50 money-making business ideas for older teens (Surrey Books, Chicago, 1990).

Better Than a Lemonade Stand, by Daryl Bernstein. Written by a 15-year-old. Describes his favorite small businesses (Beyond Words Publishing, Hillsboro, OR, 1992).

Biz Kids' Guide to Success, by Terri Thompson. Discusses how young people can make money by starting their own business (Barron's Educational Series, Hauppauge, NY, 1992).

Making Cents: Every Kid's Guide to Money, by Elizabeth Wilkinson. Shows kids how to have a good time earning money in their spare time (Little, Brown and Co., Boston, 1989).

Books on operating a service business

Kid Sitter Basics, by Celeste Stuhring, R.N. A handbook designed to help you become a better and safer babysitter (Westport Publishers, Kansas City, MO, 1-800-347-BOOK).

Bicycle Maintenance and Repair, by editors of Bicycling Magazine, a complete guide to 37 common repair jobs (Rodale Press, Emmaus, PA).

Speed Cleaning, by Jeff Campbell and The Clean Team. A step-by step anyone can understand system for cleaning the whole house (Dell Publishing, New York,1987).

Is There Life After Housework?, by Don Aslett. Step-by-step instructions for cleaning every area of the home (Writer's Digest Books, Cincinnati, OH).

Pet Clean-up Made Easy, by Don Aslett. How to clean up every kind of animal mess imaginable (Writer's Digest Books, Cincinnati, OH).

How to Make Your Own Video, by Perry Schwartz. Informative book for grades 5 and up that explains basics of video production (Lerner Publications, Minneapolis, MN).

Photography: Take Your Best Shot, by Terri Morgan and Shmuel Thaler. An outstanding trade book that teaches the fundamentals of photography (Lerner Publications, Minneapolis, MN).

Birthday Parties, by Vicki Lansky. Games, decorations, food, and themes for kids parties (Practical Parenting, Dept. 5M-89, 18326 Minnetonka Boulevard, Deephaven, MN 55391).

Great Gift Wrapping, by Burglind Neirmann. Fully illustrated instructions on basics of gift wrapping (Sterling Publishing Co, New York).

Be a Clown!, by Turk Pipkin. A lively, humerous book that covers all aspects of clownmanship, including makeup, costumes, handshakes, props, and tricks (Workman Publishing, New York).

Magic for Beginners, by Harry Baron. Over 75 magic tricks that beginners any age can learn and perform (Prima Publishing, Rocklin, CA).

Books on operating a retail business

Start Your Own Lemonade Stand, by Steven Caney. An introduction to entrepreneurship and kit for starting a lemonade stand and operating it as a successful business (Workman Publishing, New York,1991).

Baking Projects for Children, by Fran Stephens. Information on how to make gingerbread houses, decorated cakes, more (Murdoch Books, Nazareth, PA, 1993).

Mrs. Witty's Monster Cookies, by Helen Witty. Collection of award-winning recipes for making super-size cookies (Workman Publishing, New York).

The Muppets Make Puppets!, by Cheryl Henson. How to create and operate over 35 great puppets using stuff from around your house (Workman Publishing, New York,1994).

Market Guide for Young Writers, by Kathy Henderson. Guide to preparing a manuscript and addresses of over 100 publishers interested in young writers (Writer's Digest Books, Cincinnati, OH).

Potpourri, Incense and Other Fragrant Concoctions, by Ann Tucker Fettner. Everything you need to know to make your own potpourri, scented candles, sachets, and incense (Workman Publishing, New York,1977).

Pay Dirt, by Mimi Luebbermann. How to earn money raising and selling herbs and produce in your own backyard (Prima Publishing, Rocklin, CA).

The Wholesale-by-Mail Catalog, by The Print Project. Over 500 sources to shop by mail and receive 30% to 90% discount on list price (HarperCollins Publishers, New York,1995).

Books about success

Kids Can Succeed!, by Daryl Bernstein. Collection of 51 tips for overcoming real-life problems and being a success (Bob Adams, Inc., Holbrook, MA, 1993).

The Problem Solvers, by Nathan Aaseng. Collection of short biographies of famous people who turned problems into products we use today (Lerner Publications, Minneapolis, MN, 1989).

From Rags to Riches, by Nathan Aaseng. Collection of short biographies of people who started businesses from scratch and became wealthy (Lerner Publications, Minneapolis, MN, 1990).

The Rejects, by Nathan Aaseng. Collection of short stories of people whose products or inventions were rejected but who later became successful (Lerner Publications, Minneapolis, MN, 1989).

Books on careers

Careers Without College Series, developed by Peggy Schmidt. Series of 14 books on how to develop a career out of a special interest. *Examples:* music, computers, entertainment, sports, fashion, and cars (Peterson's Guides, Princeton, NJ, 1992).

A NOTE FROM THE AUTHOR

Do you have comments about this book? Do you have a story about a business? Your letters will help me do research for future books about young entrepreneurs. Write to: Bonnie Drew, 2615 Calder Drive, League City, TX 77573. Thanks!

·18·

How Adults Can Help Young Entrepreneurs

ADULTS WHO INFLUENCE THE SUCCESS OF YOUNG ENTREPRENEURS FALL INTO FOUR general categories:

1. Customers
2. Community business leaders
3. Parents
4. Educators

If you belong to one of these groups, this chapter is especially for you.

First of all, I would like to thank the parents, teachers, and community leaders who have assisted in my search for young entrepreneurs to include in this book. Without your help, I would not have met all these wonderful young people. Thank you for trusting me with your kids and allowing me to learn from you and them.

You will be interested to know that while I was interviewing the young entrepreneurs, I asked most of them to tell me what they wish adults would do to help them. I am going to share some of their answers in this chapter.

What kids wish customers would do

Friends and family are the biggest customers of young entrepreneurs. However, a number of young people find it particularly difficult to do business with friends and family. The reason is friends and family usually expect a "special deal."

Here are some of the guidelines kids wish customers would follow when doing business with young entrepreneurs:

1. Even if you are friends or family, pay us a fair wage for our work. Don't act like we're cheating you if we expect you to pay like everyone else. We can't work for free, or we'll go out of business.

2. Honor the prices we set. Kids don't like to be short-changed. We are very disappointed when adults don't live up to agreements.

3. Keep our flyers when we hand them out. It hurts to see you wad them up as you walk back in the house.

4. Be pleasant when we knock on your door. It's hard to speak to strangers who act rude or give us wierd looks.

5. Give us specific instructions about what you want done, but don't lecture. We like to feel we can ask questions if we need help.

6. We want to please you, but don't expect perfection. If you hover over us while we're working, it makes us nervous and we usually make more mistakes.

7. Call us more often. We really want to serve you.

WHAT KIDS WISH OTHER BUSINESS PEOPLE WOULD DO

Jolie Barras (Jolie's Riding School) has a hard time being taken seriously when she attends Chamber of Commerce functions because she looks so young. This is a big problem for most young entrepreneurs.

Melissa Gollick (MelMaps) conceals the fact that she's still in elementary school by communicating with realtors by fax and mail as much as possible. Jeremy Mattern (MediClaim) says it's really funny to see the reaction in a doctor's office when he first arrives to install software on the doctor's computer.

Young entrepreneurs wish other business people would take time to get to know them before they pass judgement. These are some additional ways business leaders can help young entrepreneurs:

1. We need wholesalers who will give us good prices on inventory. Help us get connections. If you are a wholesaler, give us the chance to prove we can be a reliable customer.

2. If you are a retailer, try to give our products room in your store. David Kahl (Better Letters) and Larry Villella (ConServ Sprinkler) both get support from local retailers in their communities. This makes their products more attractive to larger distributors.

3. Let us put up signs or leave flyers on your counter. The deli where Brad Boisvert (The Perfect Edible Centerpiece) worked considered him a local celebrity. They liked having Brad advertise his catering services with eye-catching signs in their deli.

4. Take time to talk to us and answer our questions seriously. Jeremy Mattern got the idea for MediClaim software from talking to his dentist. Daniel Dean (Daniel Dean Timber Co.) learned the timber-cutting business by asking questions and watching other logging crews.

5. Give us business when you can. Jeremy's dentist was the first doctor to use the MediClaim software. His feedback about the program provided valuable research.

6. Pay us the same as anyone else. Shannon Ramsey (Han-Del-Mail) says her biggest gripe is business people who try to intimidate her into lowering her rates for delivering flyers. She has learned to be very firm about her prices.

7. Be a mentor. Bill Daniels, founder of Young Americans Bank, has taken an active role in mentoring several young entrepreneurs, including Adam Fingersh (Adam F. Designs). Adam says he learned about integrity in business from watching Bill Daniels.

HOW PARENTS CAN HELP YOUNG ENTREPRENEURS

Most of the young people interviewed in this book accomplished remarkable success because they had outstanding support from their family. Without support, some would have achieved success anyway, but not as fast and probably not to the same degree.

Working with beginning entrepreneurs

One of the best ways to interest your child in entrepreneurship is to have occasional family money-making projects. These are some examples:

Raise money for a family outing by recycling cans.

Have a garage sale and let the kids keep the money from selling toys, games, and books they've outgrown.

Rent a booth at a flea market, and give the kids one table to sell craft items they've made.

Let kids to do extra, beyond-the-call-of-duty chores around the house to earn money for Christmas.

By participating in family money-making ventures, young people learn they can determine the amount of money they have to spend by the amount of work they do. They gain confidence and experience in planning a project, talking to customers, completing work on time, and handling money. With these skills, they now have options. When their allowance won't cover everything they want, they know they can earn money.

Most young entrepreneurs experiment with at least several money-making ventures before they settle down and start a serious business enterprise. The advantage of this experimentation is that they learn a great deal about their talents, skills, and work styles. As long as young people complete current work that is due a customer, there is no harm in changing ventures as often as they wish.

Parents would be wise, however, to set a few basic rules about these business ventures:

Schoolwork always comes first.

Loans for start-up money must be paid back.

Shoddy work will be done over for free.

If you start a job, you have to complete it.

Dishonesty will result in loss of privileges.

As long as young entrepreneurs are not spending money on anything harmful or illegal, the money they earn should be theirs to spend as they please. They will learn even more about budgeting money if you refuse to lend money when they run out. For more on this subject, read my previous book titled *MoneySkills: 101 Activities to Teach Your Child about Money* (Career Press, 1992).

Working with talented young entrepreneurs

It's not hard to recognize born entrepreneurs. They are the ones you find going up and down the street at age 5 or 6, selling painted rocks, kindergarten pictures, frogs, or coat hangers. They initiate money-making ventures without prodding from parents. Although most of them enjoy having money to spend, money is not their primary motivation. They are motivated by the opportunity for self-expression. Sometimes it's difficult for parents to understand the talented and gifted young person. These kids run on a different "track" than other kids. They have an inner guidance system leading them on a mission far beyond the scope of normal vision. And they are usually too young to tell you what they are doing. They just have to do it.

This book is full of stories of young people like this. I feel privileged to know them. Often when I am interviewing them, I wonder if I am speaking to a future Steve Jobs, Bill Gates, Debbi Fields, or Oprah Winfrey. I like to think I may be helping them toward their ultimate goals.

If you are a parent or teacher of a talented and gifted young person, read biographies of famous people whose remarkable accomplishments changed the world. The reading lists in Chapters 17 and 18 include several of my favorite books on this subject. These books will help you understand and support the development of your gifted child's talents.

From my work with young entrepreneurs of all ages and stages, these are my suggestions for ways you can encourage the growth of business talent:

1. *Give them a computer or access to a computer as early as possible.* A computer is essential for running a business today. Most of these kids pick up computerese very quickly. Brian Wood (MediClaim) remembers getting his first computer at age 3. For him, programming was natural. He says, "I wanted to make the computer do things, so I read the manuals and taught myself. I've known how to program for so long, it's hard to remember what it's like not to know. It seems like I've always known."

2. *Help them get whatever equipment they need.* Music instruments are essential to develop a talent in music. Tools are essential for a child who is talented in mechanics. If you can't afford the equipment, work with your child to earn the money to get it.

3. *Give them space to work.* Steven Schecter's parents gave him half the basement for a music room. (The other half is his sister's.) Some parents also share office space and office equipment. Brad Boisvert's mom shares her kitchen. Brad does all his baking and catering jobs right out of their normal-size home kitchen.

4. *Share your business knowledge as the kids are ready to listen.* When Jordan Levine and his friend Josh Vinitz started Odd Ball Enterprises, Jordan's dad helped them write contracts and gave them advice about sales. Until then, Jordan wasn't interested in dad's business ideas. It's best to wait until the kids ask for advice before you try to give it.

5. *Partner with them if necessary.* Tamara Pechon's mother signed up as an Avon representative so Tamara could sell products at school. Nick Batchelor's grandfather helped him start Nick's Nacks by supplying inventory left over from another store he had owned. But more than that, Nick's grandfather is teaching him how to run a store.

6. *Be careful about lending your child money.* Kids are very convincing when it comes to getting loans. They are also very unreliable about paying back. A loan can be a source of big problems between parents and kids. Know your child well, and make all loan agreements in writing. If your child does not live up to the agreement, don't give any more loans for at least 6 months.

7. *Honor your kid's business decisions.* When Tommy Tighe (Kids for Peace) got letters from a class of 37 students in Pennsylvania who wanted to sell his bumper stickers, Tommy's mother told him he could write one letter back to the whole class. Although he was very busy in school, Tommy insisted on writing every kid a personal letter. When the kids got their letters, they were so excited they were chanting his name in the halls after school.

8. *Don't over-emphasize the money they make.* They would rather be praised for their good ideas or how much they helped a customer. Jason Miller (JM Industries) says interviewers on radio and TV have tried to force him to tell how much he earns with his computer business. His only answer is, "I make enough."

9. *Use your connections to get your kids ahead.* Evan Robert's mother wrote the theme song for the *DynaMet* TV show, then requested that the producers audition Evan for a part as a sportscaster. Julie Neubauer (Julie's Crafty T's) was able to start teaching community education classes at age 13 because her mother had been teaching at the center and knew the director.

10. *Don't neglect the rest of the family.* Involve them in support. Evan Roberts relies on his older sister to help him study scripts. His dad teaches him sports history and helps him memorize statistics. His mother does publicity. Evan gives everyone in the family an equal share of every paycheck he gets. He is quick to tell anyone who asks about his success that he couldn't do it without his family.

How Educators Can Help Young Entrepreneurs

Students today want to know how their classwork relates to the real world. Entrepreneurship is an ideal way to tie almost any subject into practical life experience. It is also a wonderful tool for team teaching.

Running a business takes math skills to figure profits, make correct change, manage a bank account, compute hourly wage, estimate expenses, and figure sales tax. English skills are used to write business letters, compose press releases, and write advertising material. Science classes learn how the inventing process includes finding a market for the product. Social studies and economics classes learn about the free enterprise system and how the stock market operates. Students enrolled in technology courses such as careers, home economics, and computers learn ways to market the skills they acquire in the classroom.

The most effective way to offer students a multi-disciplinary learning experience is to operate short-term business enterprises in the classroom. These are some suggestions for group money-making projects:

Compose and publish a cookbook.

Run a bike clinic; teach bicycle safety and repair.

Operate a video rental service.

Operate a toy and game rental service.

Run a Saturday sitting service.

Sell craft items such as potpourri or T-shirts.

Have a chili dinner or pancake breakfast.

Publish a school directory.

Have a used-book sale.

Repair donated toys and have a toy sale.

Build the world's largest fudge sundae and sell it.

Publish a coupon book for discounts at local businesses.

Put on a play or workshop and sell tickets.

Sell pretzels or subs at football games.

Sponsor a talent show or a battle of the bands.

Host a kids' flea market, and charge kids to exhibit.

Do a class or group recycling project.

Get corporate sponsors for a neighborhood cleanup.

Sponsor a baseball card show.

In addition to these ideas, many of the 101 businesses described in this book can be adapted to the classroom or used for fund-raising activities for youth organizations. These business ventures are also particularly helpful for special education classes and for school-to-work transition programs.

Probably the most difficult task teachers or youth leaders have is helping students learn to write business plans. Kids aren't excited about business plans. They are excited about being entrepreneurs.

Teaching the business plan doesn't have to be boring. Here are several ways to make it more fun:

1. Use stories of contemporary entrepreneurs as case studies as you teach the components of the business plan.

2. Invite business owners or other young entrepreneurs to speak in the classroom.

3. Send the students out into the community to interview real business people about business planning.

Teachers can also use *Fast Cash for Kids* as a complete guide for an entrepreneurship course. This entire book has been written with the purpose of teaching correct business procedures while keeping business students interested and excited about becoming entrepreneurs.

EDUCATIONAL RESOURCES

In addition to the organizations listed in Chapter 17, teachers and parents will find the following resources helpful:

Center for Education and Training for Employment, Ohio State University, 1900 Kenny Road Columbus, OH 43210 (1-800-848-4815). Request information on *PACE (Program for Acquiring Competence in Entrepreneurship),* a series of student modules and teacher's guides for teaching business skills. Join the International Consortium for Entrepreneurship Education and receive 30% off all PACE materials. You will also receive an excellent newsletter called *EntrepreNews & Views.* Dr. M. Catherine Ashmore is director.

Children's Financial Network, Inc., Neale S. Godfrey, Chairman, 70 Tower Hill Road, Mountain Lakes, NJ 07046. Request information on books and materials to teach young people about money, banking, and business.

EMC Publishing, 300 York Avenue, St. Paul, MN 55101 (1-800-328-1452). Request information on a teacher's guide titled *Risks & Rewards of Entrepreneurship* by M. Catherine Ashmore, which helps young people assess their suitability for business ownership.

I Have a Dream—Houston, Carrol G. Peery, Executive Director, P.O. Box 541183, Houston, TX 77254 (713-523-7326). Request information on the Houston Tree Kids project to teach kids how to operate a business and give them opportunity to earn their own money while improving the environment.

Illinois Institute for Entrepreneurship Education, Attn: Thomas E. Murray, Ed.D., 28 E. Jackson, Suite 1220, Chicago, IL 60604. Request information about teacher-training workshops on entrepreneurship available at Northern Illinois University.

Media Crafters Limited, Don Maynard, President, 7201 Haven Avenue, Suite E-325, Alta Loma, CA 91701 (1-800-874-6884). zst ordering information for a video titled *Kids Venture: How to Start Your Own Business.* Appropriate for grades 6 to 8.

Minnesota Extension Service Distribution Center, University of Minnesota, 1420 Eckles Avenue, St. Paul, MN 55108. Request information on *Y.E.S.* curriculum guides for teaching youth entrepreneurship. Sample topics are personal assessment, community assessment, and how to write a business plan.

North Central College, Students in Free Enterprise, 30 N. Brainard, Naperville, IL 60566. Request information on the award-winning educational game "Where's the Dough?" created by college students to teach high school students how to start a business.

North Dakota State University Area Extension Specialist, Kathleen Tweenten, 514 East Thayer Avenue, Bismarck, ND 58501 (701-221-6865). Request information on *Be Your Own Boss* youth entrepreneurship curriculum for grades 5 to 8. Includes 10 weeks of lessons and numerous visual aids.

Oklahoma Department of Vocational and Technical Education, 1500 West Seventh Avenue, Stillwater, OK 74074 (1-800-654-4502). Request information on curriculum for teaching marketing and entrepreneurship to grades 6 to 8. Supplements to this curriculum are Bonnie Drew's book *Fast Cash for Kids* and *Kids Business Software.*

Oklahoma REAL Enterprises, Inc., Attn: Denise Coldwater, P.O. Box 100, Forgan, OK 73938. Request information about their pilot project to teach entrepreneurship to rural students at four campuses through interactive television.

Oklahoma Small Business Development Center at Northwestern Oklahoma State University (OSBDC at NWSU), 709 Oklahoma Boulevard, Alva, OK 73717 (405-327-5883). Contact Connie Murrell, Regional Director, for information on youth entrepreneurship workshops she has organized and presented at various schools in northwest Oklahoma.

Pacific Bell Directory, Communications Deptartment. CWS7, 101 Spear Street, Room 429, San Francisco, CA 94105 (1-800-848-8000). Request free issues of magazine, *Small Business Success,* which contain numerous articles on business management and extensive lists of business resources.

U.S. Small Business Administration, Office of Advocacy, Mail Code 3114, 409 Third Street SW, Washington, DC 20416 (202-205-6941). This agency advocates legislation that assists young entrepreneurs. Request information on how to participate in the annual Small Business Person of the Year award nominations.

RECOMMENDED READING

For Entrepreneurs Only, by Wilson Harrell. Inspirational ideas and success strategies for anyone starting or growing a business (Career Press, Hawthorne, NJ, 1994).

Homemade Money, 5th edition, by Barbara Brabec. The definitive guide to success with a home-based business (Betterway Books, Crozet, VA).

The Lemonade Stand, by Emmanuel Modu. A how-to guide for encouraging the entrepreneur in every child (Bob Adams, Inc., Holbrook, MA, 1991).

Profiles of Female Genius, by Gene N. Landrum. Explores common personality characteristics of 13 contemporary women who changed the world (Prometheus Books, Amherst, NY, 1994).

Profiles of Genius, by Gene N. Landrum. Studies of the lives of 13 men who became business giants and changed the world (Prometheus Books, Amherst, NY 1993).

Our Wildest Dreams: Women Entrepreneurs Making Money, Having Fun, Doing Good, by Joline Godfrey. A whole new definition integrity and business ethics (HarperBusiness, New York, NY, 1992).

Kiplinger's Money-Smart Kids (and parents, too), by Janet Bodnar. How to turn your kids into super-savers, smart shoppers, and cautious users of credit (Kiplinger Books, Washington, DC, 1993).

MoneySkills: 101 Activites to Teach Your Child about Money, by Bonnie Drew. Everyday games and activities to make it fun for kids age 3 to12 to learn to save, spend, and budget money (Career Press, Hawthorne, NJ, 1992).

· INDEX ·